970.3 Karen, Ruth
KAR
      Song of the quail

DATE			
signature			

SONG OF THE QUAIL

SONG OF THE

THE WONDROUS WORLD OF THE MAYA

FOUR WINDS PRESS, NEW YORK

QUAIL

Ruth Karen

By the same author

THE LAND AND PEOPLE OF CENTRAL AMERICA

NEIGHBORS IN A NEW WORLD: THE ORGANIZATION OF AMERICAN STATES

THE SEVEN WORLDS OF PERU

HELLO GUATEMALA

Title page: a classic Maya figure, emerging from a water lily.
The clay figure is from the island of Jaina, in Mexico.
MUSEUM OF PRIMITIVE ART, NEW YORK

Published by Four Winds Press
A Division of Scholastic Magazines, Inc., New York, N.Y.
Copyright © 1972 by Ruth Karen
All rights reserved.
Printed in the United States of America
Library of Congress Catalogue Card Number: 75–182110

0 9 8 7 6 5 4 3 2

FOR BARRY

CONTENTS

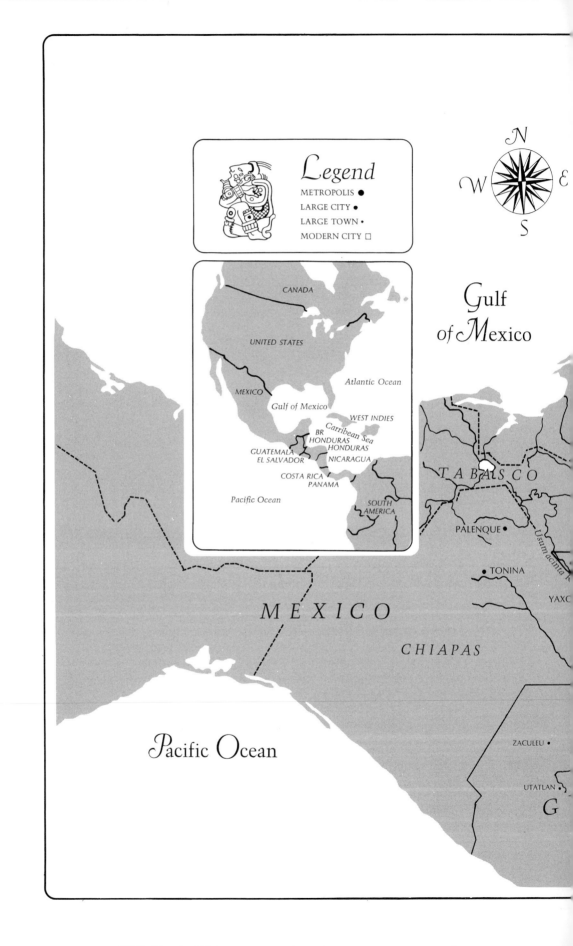

Legend

METROPOLIS ●
LARGE CITY ●
LARGE TOWN ·
MODERN CITY ☐

CANADA

UNITED STATES

Atlantic Ocean

MEXICO

Gulf of Mexico

WEST INDIES

Carribean Sea

BR
HONDURAS
HONDURAS

GUATEMALA
EL SALVADOR

NICARAGUA

COSTA RICA
PANAMA

SOUTH
AMERICA

Pacific Ocean

Gulf
of Mexico

T A B A S C O

PALENQUE ·

Usumacinta R

· TONINA

YAXC

M E X I C O

C H I A P A S

Pacific Ocean

ZACULEU ·

UTATLAN ·

G

PART I

1: THE TEMPLES OF TIKAL

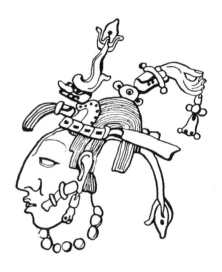

TWO HOURS FROM MIAMI, FLORIDA, AS THE JET FLIES—ALTHOUGH no jet lands as yet on the short and often soggy Tikal airstrip that has been hacked out of the rainforest—a thousand year old temple rises twenty stories high, to point like a finger in humanity's long reach for the universe. The temple, with a base constructed like a pyramid, but crowned with a carved roofcomb that looks like a monumental version of the decoration Spanish dancers wear in their hair, was erected by the Maya, the wondrous Indian people who created one of the three major civilizations that existed in the Americas when Columbus came.

The other two civilizations were established by the Inca and the Aztec. The Inca, from their capital at Cuzco in the high Andes, ruled an empire that encompassed all of what today is Peru, stretched north to Ecuador, south to Chile, east to parts of Bolivia and the Argentine and west to the shores of the Pacific. The Inca embraced in their empire a number of other Indian civilizations of South America that had preceded them in time and, in some aspects, had surpassed them in achievement.

The Aztec, when the first Europeans encountered them, held sway in North America, the part that is now Central Mexico. Like the Inca, they were conquerers of a fairly recent vintage, having subdued, through warfare or enforced alliance, other important civilizations that flourished before them.

The Maya's realm was Middle America, stretching from the Yucatan Peninsula through the Central American isthmus, including what now are the southern Mexican states of Yucatan, Quintana Roo, Campeche and Tabasco as well as Guatemala, Honduras, British Honduras and parts of El Salvador. At its peak—in the second half of the first millennium of our calendar—the Maya realm encompassed some 125,000 square miles and a population estimated at about fifteen million. Unlike the Inca and the Aztec areas, however, the Maya realm was not an empire but an association of city-states, each with its own temporal and spiritual ruler. These leaders respected and honored each other, exchanged knowledge and goods, and shared an abstract but carefully defined concept of the laws of the universe and man's role in that universe.

While the Inca were superb social organizers, and the Aztec powerful warriors, thus combining between them the strength that made Rome the master of ancient Europe, the Maya were comparable to the Greeks. Their inspiration was not a lust for power but a desire for harmony, and their achievements were not in the skills of war

*A stele, with figures and glyphs,
from the Maya city-state of
Piedras Negras, in Guatemala.*
UNIVERSITY MUSEUM,
UNIVERSITY OF PENNSYLVANIA

The haunting faces of Maya
sculpture: This is a young god,
carved in stone, from Honduras.
UNIVERSITY MUSEUM,
UNIVERSITY OF PENNSYLVANIA

The Maya also sculpted in jadeite, a
rough marbled form of jade found
in the Guatemalan highlands.
This famous jadeite head comes
from Tikal.

and the devices of administration, but—as with the Greeks—in the arts and the sciences.

The Maya built magnificently. Their sacred cities rivaled Egypt in splendor and Greece in grace. They painted exquisitely in colors both vivid and subtle, depicting figures and objects that are natural as well as elegant. They sculptured superbly, in high relief and low, intricate designs and haunting faces that can still be encountered throughout the Mayan area.

In the sciences, their greatest achievements were astronomy and calendrics, mathematics and the invention of a written language.

A sculpture in ceramic: the god of cocoa, from Guatemala.
UNIVERSITY MUSEUM, UNIVERSITY OF PENNSYLVANIA

Observatories were scattered in strategic locations throughout the Mayan realm and the priest-scientists who attended them regularly exchanged information. As a result, the Maya, more than a thousand years ago, had tracked the course of the planet Venus as accurately as scientists, with their radar, laser beams and giant telescopes do today.

The Maya devised three calendars—a sacred, a natural, and a planetary one—and used the three as a kind of check on each other. Mayan mathematical concepts surpassed in sophistication those of their contemporaries in Europe (they invented the notion of zero long before Europe learned it from the Arabs). And they were the only people in the Americas to have created an original written language, consisting of a myriad of glyphs and ideograms most of which have not yet been deciphered.

The Maya are often described as "the mysterious Maya." This is because we have encountered many of their achievements but are still baffled by the systems and techniques that made these achievements possible. As yet we do not know what made Maya civilization flourish as it did, nor what caused it to decay. We do know that it spanned a period of close to 3,000 years, including a Golden Age that lasted for five centuries at a time when Europe was lost in its Dark Ages.

At Tikal, where palaces and ball courts; houses and altars; water reservoirs, storage bins and steam baths; tombs and tall stone monuments covered with glyphs and faces (archeologists call these stelae); and a score of temples have been unearthed in recent years, the imagination is tempted to fill in scenes to cover the giant gaps in knowledge. One can picture the city on a holiday like the first day of the month of Chen, when the images of new household gods were

A Maya priest-scientist, kneeling and deep in thought. The figure, said to have been found near the Tabasco-Guatemala border, is carved from wood.
MUSEUM OF PRIMITIVE ART, NEW YORK

A temple pyramid of Tikal as it is peeled out of the jungle.

This is another building in Tikal, before it was uncovered.

welcomed to the home like honored guests and installed in their niches. The gods were fashioned by artists dedicated to the making of icons. The craftsmen worked silently and abstinently in stone chambers set aside for them on temple grounds. By the first of Chen, they had completed their task for the year and the entire city joined them in celebration. Families thronged into the center from the farms that radiated from Tikal's core into the jungle. Visitors came from other cities and lands. Among them were ambassadors, recognizable by the feather fans they carried, the size and splendor of which indicated their rank, and by the exotic presents they brought to express their admiration of the *halach uinic*, the "true man," who ruled Tikal.

At such time of festivity, many merchants came to the market with their wares: tools of flint and obsidian; clay bowls, plates, jars and vases covered with many colors and high glazes; feathers of the parrot, the trogon, the toucan, for making mantles and headbands; jaguar pelts for breechclouts; sandals, logwood dye, copal incense; spices, including the tongue-burning chili and the fragrant vanilla; jade from the highlands and gold from the south; rubber for balls used in the sacred *pok-to-pok* game and for the players' belts, masks and knee guards; and, from the coast, shells and stingrays, turtles and dried fish. Coin of the realm was the cacao bean and the copper bell. Both glinted brown and mellow under the tropical sun and made a gentle sound as they were counted out in trade.

Over the causeways leading to the city, nobles arrived from their estates, or from smaller outlying towns, carried in litters of wood or pelt covered by canopies of plumes. In the limestone-paved streets of the city, swept clean and glowing white, musicians marched in procession, blowing trumpets, playing flutes, beating drums, and piercing the air with rhythmic sounds from their conch shells. In the

A temple pyramid in the days of Tikal's glory. Restoration drawing by Tatiana Proskouriakoff

And what remains of it today. PEABODY MUSEUM, HARVARD UNIVERSITY

plazas, dancers, dressed in elaborate costumes and holding colored banners, moved steadily and gracefully in large circles. In two or three of the ballcourts, games of *pok-to-pok* held spectators enthralled.

High above the main plaza, priests in flowing white robes emerged from their sacristies atop the temples to celebrate the ritual of the day. Twenty stories below, the throngs watched in devout silence.

Worship, ballgames, dance and music over, the feasting began. Eating mats were piled high with game and fruit, accompanied by jugs of "honeyfire," a fermented drink made of the wild bee's honey, cacao, and a dash of chili, swizzled into a foamy beverage that tasted sweet and sharp. It was not polite on such occasions to abandon the feast before dawn, and it was considered rude to fall asleep. To this day, descendants of the Maya celebrate religious occasions with a combination of devotion and festivity that ends at dawn, when the church bell tolls. In the days of Tikal's glory the town crier probably announced the end of the feast with a rattle topped by feathers, his badge of office.

But what spelled the end of all feasting for Tikal? What caused this magnificent metropolis to be abandoned, as apparently it was sometime in the ninth century, leaving its temples to be obscured once more by the treetops, its houses to molder until nothing remained but the slight elevations on which they had been built, its altars to crack, the stelae smashed or crumbling and covered with roots and lianas?

As yet, there is no certain answer. Some scientists believe that the soil gave out. The leached, poor topsoil of the tropical rainforest, which the Maya burnt down to plant their crops, could no longer feed the people of the metropolis, and hunger caused the desertion of the city. Others say that a sickness, one of many to which the debilitating tropical climate gives rise, swept Tikal and decimated its people. Still others hold that the reason lay in the civilization itself. It had become too refined, this theory maintains. The ruling caste of priests, nobles, and scientists had become too removed from the populace and its daily concerns to make for a viable community. The people, no longer understanding the abstractions of their rulers, felt no relationship to these men at the top and no longer saw the need to feed them, or to build for them. And the peak of the social pyramid could not exist without the sustaining base. Having lost its inner mortar of relationship and cohesion, the city crumbled and disappeared into the murky unknown from which it had sprung.

Whether Tikal had been a ritual center, a kind of Jerusalem of the jungle to which worshipers thronged for special occasions, or a true city like New York, London or Tokyo in which people lived, worked and worshiped, has not yet been determined either.

Nor has anyone yet been able to account for the unprecedented feat of such a civilization having been created in such surroundings. Most of the world's great civilizations—the Sumerians and the Greeks, the Babylonians and the Egyptians, the Persians and the Medes, the heart of the civilizations of China and India—evolved in moderate climates or, if they were created in a hotter temperature, in an open valley, along the banks of a river. The only other jungle civilizations we know, those of Java and Cambodia, were brought to the rainforest already fully developed, and did not long endure. In Tikal, a civilization was wrested from the jungle, built slowly over the centuries, and lasted in glory for five hundred years.

What kind of people did this? What do we know about them?

II: SONG
OF
THE QUAIL

KNOWLEDGE OF THE EARLIEST ORIGINS OF THE MAYA IS, EVEN more than with most peoples, a mixture of guesswork and myth. The guesswork is logical and intriguing, but neither dependable nor definitive. The myths are appealing and colorful, reflecting the attempt of a people, early concerned with human and universal harmony, to find a pattern that would make moral sense of the relationship of man to man, and philosophical sense of the relationship of man to nature. As the Maya experienced it, nature was a complex phenomenon, with its life-sustaining plants and animals and unpredictable rains and floods, its torrential storms and volcanic eruptions, and its reassuring heavens with their orderly processions of dawns and dusks, suns, moons, planets and stars.

26

The guesswork reaches back about 10,000 years when, scientists speculate, a solid bridge of ice spanned what are now the waters of the Bering Strait between Siberia and Alaska. Across this frozen highway wandered tribes and groups of northeast Asians into what are now the Americas. Some settled down after crossing the ice bridge and learned to make a life amid the snow. These are the Aleuts of Alaska. Others pushed on south until they reached a warmer climate and inviting plains that seemed to stretch from horizon to horizon. These wanderers became the Indians of the middle section of the United States, whose civilizations never grew much beyond the nomadic hunting stage.

A few of the Asian wanderers were lured further south, perhaps by the warmth, perhaps by curiosity and a sense of adventure. Just what drives some peoples to the challenging complexities of creating civilizations, while others seem to come and go leaving little or no evidence of their existence, remains a puzzle of mankind. In the Americas, we know that the further south these wanderers went, the more ambitious they became. In North America, they began to evolve cultures in Arizona and New Mexico. Those that moved on further to what is now Mexico proper built the luxuriant civilizations of the Olmecs, the Toltecs, the Mixtecs and Zapotecs, and the Aztecs. Further still from their Asian origins, in the Andean highlands and along the Pacific coast of South America, the Chavin and the Tehuanaco, the Moche, the Nazca, the Paracas, and finally the Inca shaped societies whose arts and achievements impress and delight us still. Between the two massive continents, on that curving little isthmus which on a map looks like a curled serpent with a large triangular head, the Maya achieved their triumphs.

One fantastic theory maintained for some time that all of South

America is really the lost continent of Atlantis. Believers in this theory contended that convolutions of the earth did not sweep Atlantis under the sea but tossed it up, high above the earth's crust, to form the Andean peaks. The civilizations that developed amidst these forbidding crests and crags, that theory argued, had really flowered earlier on Atlantis, when that lost continent was a low, large island floating in the pleasant breezes of the South Atlantic.

As for the Maya, there were people, serious scholars among them, who held that these marvelous people of the American jungle were really the lost ten tribes of Israel. This proposition had the advantage of accounting both for what had happened to those famous tribes, and for the inspiration that had made possible the marvels created by the Maya.

The latest hypotheses about the true origin of America's earliest settlers are based on recent discoveries of human remains which carbon tests have shown to be around 17,000 years old. This causes archeologists to speculate whether the migrations from Asia to America took place earlier than the 10,000 years they had thought, as much as seven millennia earlier. It proves primarily just how patchy our knowledge still is.

One thing we do know with reasonable certainty is that those early Americans who kept trekking south, beyond the central plains of North America, discovered or developed corn three or four thousand years ago. We know also that having made this discovery, they learned to cultivate the crop and settled down in agricultural communities. Between harvest and planting time, the people of these communities found themselves, for the first time in their history, with the precious gift of leisure, time in which to turn their minds to things other than physical survival. We know also that these agricultural communities kept people settled in one place, or at least a small range of places. Now, the curiosity and spirit of adventure which had prompted their long migration had to find outlet in a different kind of search, a search that went beyond the challenges of the nomad's changing environment. They began to build a civilization.

Maya myths tell a different tale of these prehistoric beginnings. As in most other religions, it is a story of paradise lost.

The Maya myths of creation have come down to us in a book called the *Popol Vuh*, which recounts the experience, from the creation of the earth until the Spanish conquest and a few generations thereafter, of one of the major Maya tribes, the Quiche of the Guatemalan highlands. We know what the *Popol Vuh* says because it was written down, in the Quiche language but in Latin characters, by one of the Quiche princes who had survived the Spanish conquest and had been educated in a Spanish school. *Popol Vuh* means the Book of Council or the Book of the Community, the word *popol* deriving from *pop*, the woven mat on which Maya elders, judges and counselors sat when public issues were debated. Translators and historians have since referred to the *Popol Vuh* as the Sacred Book of the Maya. It was the Maya equivalent to the Old Testament.

According to these sacred scriptures, four perfect human beings were created to begin the Maya race. Three of their names contained the word *balam*, which means jaguar. To the Maya, the jaguar was a symbol of power.

"These are the names of the first men who were created and formed," says the *Popol Vuh*. "The first man was Balam-Quiche, the second Balam-Acab, the third Mahacutah, and the fourth was Iqui-Balam. These are the names of our first mothers and fathers."

The myth of how these first ancestors were created bears a close resemblance to the concept of man's creation in the Old Testament. They were fashioned out of nothing, by the word of God.

This is how the *Popol Vuh* puts it :

"They were made and formed. They had no mother, they had no father. They were called men. . . . By a miracle, by means of incantation, were they created and made by the Creator."

Thereafter, the two Bibles diverge. In the Old Testament, Adam was a simple, innocent man living with only his natural instincts in a perfect world. In the *Popol Vuh*, the first men were perfect, all-knowing, with complete comprehension of the universe of which they were a part. In the Maya civilization, paradise was not so much a place but a time, when man understood the world and its ways.

"They [these first men] were endowed with intelligence," says the *Popol Vuh*.

They saw, and instantly they could see far. Thy succeeded in seeing. They succeeded in knowing all there is in the world. When they looked, instantly they saw all around them, and they contemplated in turn the arch of the heaven and the round face of the earth.

The things hidden in the distance they saw, without having to move. At once they saw the world, whole. From where they were, they saw it.

Great was their wisdom. Their sight reached to the forests, the rocks, the lakes, the seas, the mountains and the valleys. In truth they were admirable men, Balam-Quiche, Balam-Acab, Mahucutah, and Iqui-Balam.

Still, they fell from grace. Not as in the Old Testament by yielding to temptation, but through the jealousy of the gods who decided that they did not, after all, want to people the earth with equals. So the Maya gods obscured the sight of man.

"Then the Heart of Heaven blew mist into their eyes, which clouded their sight as when a mirror is breathed upon. Their eyes were covered and they could see only what was close, only that was clear to them.

"In this way the wisdom and all the knowledge of the four men, the origin and the beginning of the Quiche race, were destroyed."

Another Maya chronicle that has survived, the Annals of the Cakchiquels, picks up the story from there and takes it to the time when the Maya settled in the land where they and their way of life survive to this day.

The Cakchiquels were a Maya tribe which, after extensive wandering, probably south from Mexico, settled in the highlands of Guatemala, some distance from the Quiché. Like the *Popol Vuh*, the chronicle of the Cakchiquels was preserved after the Spanish conquest by being passed on verbally for several generations, and finally written down in Latin characters.

The Annals of the Cakchiquels say:

"Through clouds, through mist, through mud, through the darkness and the rain we arrived . . . where the song of the quail was heard under the tall pine trees."

III: RISE
AND FALL

ARCHEOLOGISTS DIVIDE THE HISTORY OF MAYA CIVILIZATION INTO
five segments.

First, the time of "the clouds, the mist," which archeologists call
the pre-formative period. The historic darkness of this period is such
that we do not yet know for certain whether it began in the second
millennium or the first millennium B.C. All we know is that it
ended about five hundred years before the Christian era.

The second segment of Maya history begins around 500 B.C.
and ends about 300 A.D. Archeologists call it the formative period.

Formation flowered into the luxuriance of the Golden Age.
Archeologists call this the classic period and set its time range
as 300–900 A.D.

32

The fourth segment is the period known as the New Empire, when the Maya, who had originally come from the north, trekked back there, mainly to the Yucatan Peninsula, and created a short-lived renaissance of their Golden Age. It had much of the grace and gentleness of the classic period, but little of its grandeur. It lasted less than 200 years.

The New Empire was followed by the fifth segment of Maya civilization, the segment archeologists call the Mexican period. It was a time of intermingling between the Maya and their northern neighbors. This association had begun earlier with trade and cultural exchange but degenerated into what turned out to be five hundred years of piecemeal conquest by the Toltecs, then the dominant people of Mexico.

Outright Mexican conquest never reached south of the Yucatan Peninsula. The subjugation of the Maya of the Central American isthmus was completed by the Spaniards early in the sixteenth century, most of it in a single year, 1524. Eyewitness accounts exist of the Spanish conquest, and archeologists yield to the historians when written records become available. The archeologists' mapping of the rise and fall of Maya civilization ends when the conquistadors landed.

The first visual evidence extant of Maya civilization dates from the archeologists' second segment, the formative period. This evidence comes to us from the highland Maya, the ones who heard the song of the quail under the tall pine trees. It is on the outskirts of what today is Guatemala City, a pyramid called Kaminaljuyu. The pyramid is covered with sun-dried mud and trees with gnarled roots that seem to clutch the treasure beneath as though unwilling to let go of it. On weekends, children from the surrounding suburbs

Maya artistry has early origins.
These two clay figures date from the
"formative" period, the Maya's
earliest days which are so far back in
history that we only have
approximate dates: 2000–500 B.C.
The figures were found at
Kaminaljuyu, on the outskirts of
Guatemala City.

hunt amid the trees and rocks for souvenirs from the people who lived there 2,000 years ago. They find some, such as little, rose-brown clay figurines, their features outlined clumsily, but sporting already large round rings in their ears and quite elaborate crowns of feathers on their heads. The children also find carefully shaped vessels, round bowls and long vases, and flutes and pipes made of clay. Each of these instruments is usually in the form of a mythical animal, with holes down its middle from which a tune can be coaxed.

Another signpost to the formative period rises in the jungle, not far from Tikal, at Uaxactun (Wah-shuk-toon).

The Maya rarely destroyed a place of worship. When they thought they wanted a new temple, their instinct was to build it on top of an existing one, using the old edifice as foundation and fill for the new. In some places, the last of the temples have been found to contain three and even four earlier houses of worship, each with its own ritual steps leading to temple platforms, flanked usually by carved masks and glyphs.

At Uaxactun, the innermost temple pyramid dates from the formative period. It is small compared to later Mayan edifices, only about twenty-seven feet in height. When it was first dug out from its superimposed successors, it was covered with a heavy coat of eggshell-colored stucco, "dazzling bright in the clear tropical sunlight." The description comes from one of the most famous Maya scholars, J. Eric S. Thompson, who saw the pyramid of Uaxactún very soon after it was excavated, and remembers it as "one of the most impressive and touching sights I have ever seen—this pyramid bathed in the light of a full moon. The towering trees of the uncut forest surrounding the little court in which it stood created a backdrop of black velvet for its brilliantly stuccoed mass."

The eighteen carved masks flanking its stairways, man-tall and even wider than high, represent a mythical mixture of the two animals that seem to have haunted the Maya imagination most: jaguar and serpent. Yet, the fearful features of both animals are already combined in such a way that they leave an impression of harmony, acceptance, and peace.

The next time segment brought to maturity the beginnings made at Kaminaljuyu and Uaxactun. This was the classic period, the time when Europe's Dark Ages were counterpointed on the other side of the Atlantic by the Mayas' Golden Age. During this period the Maya developed their writing. They made books, painting the glpyhs, ideograms, and illustrations on the bark of the wild fig tree, which they had processed into parchment. They also carved their glyphs in stucco or stone—brilliant white limestone or soft rose and beige sandstone—on the banisters of their temple staircases, and on the stelae and altars that studded their temple courtyards. In this classic period architecture became increasingly sophisticated. With vaulted, false arches, Mayan builders erected structures designed for meditation, for worship and for artistic creation. These edifices combined the soaring feeling of a Gothic window with the contained intimacy of a cell. Finally, astronomy flourished in this period, along with mathematics and calendrics.

As far as we know, during the 600 years of the Golden Age there never existed a single imperial ruler who held the Maya world together by force. Each city, or group of cities, was governed by its *halach uinic*, who combined civic and religious functions and was, in turn, advised and aided by priests and nobles. The priests were responsible for science, scholarship, and ritual; the nobles for administration, taxation, and community welfare. The system appears to

Monuments from the Golden Age of Maya civilization, all from Quirigua: A stele, covered with glyphs.

A stele, with a figure of a halach uinic, sculpted in high relief.

An altar top and the carved head of a jaguar. UNITED FRUIT COMPANY

have worked very smoothly indeed, with friction limited to an occasional dispute over boundaries, culminating in a day or two of battle or a brief raid. What made this extraordinary, unenforced peace possible over an area of 125,000 square miles and a period of six centuries was a shared sense of values. Rulers and ruled throughout Mayadom saw the meaning of life, the function of the individual, and the place of man in the universe, in much the same way. All accepted their part in the scheme and tried to play their roles as best they could. Perfection was important to them, and took many forms. A perfect ear of corn was as real a contribution to society, and fulfillment for the man who produced it, as was a perfect sculpture or a perfect astronomical equation. The sacred calendar, with its ordained succession of lucky and unlucky days, its predictable presents of joy and sorrow, failure and success, set the tone for everyone's life. The system made vanity absurd, and triumph of any kind a gift calling for gratitude. It left only the pride of achievement, and even that was muted by humility.

Eric Thompson, looking back over this period, sees:

An area studded with countless ceremonial centers, varying in size from those comprising four thatched hut temples atop simple platforms enclosing a court scarcely fifty feet in each direction to vast masses of platforms and pyramids, palaces and temples, rising jaggedly like granaries in Iowa or grouped with the architectural harmony of an Andalusian city.

The country around, one visualizes as a patchwork of forest, clear acres, and land reverting to forest, with the first the dominant factor, and here and there the thatched huts of the peasants grouped in fours and fives in clearings shaded by fruit trees, those of the priests and other aristocrats clustered on the outskirts of the ceremonial centers. These last might be empty, but should you return tomorrow, you would find them filled with crowds present for some ceremony or for market; and visiting them again a month hence, when the corn needs little attention, you might see files of men, women, and children carrying rocks and earth for the enlargement of a pyramid, and masons and carpenters busy laying yet more stone walls or stairways or cutting lintels or crossties for yet another temple.

One place where one can still get an intense feeling of what life must have been like in these days of glory is Copan, a city of Mayan ruins hidden in the hills of Honduras. A river curls through a broad valley between low mountain ranges; everything is moist, verdant. A plane landing, or a jeep coming to the valley by road, finds the soft earth clinging to its wheels. The river seems to have been the undulating border of a ceremonial center in which every structure, and its relationship to other structures, was mathematically calculated. The main plaza, a brilliant white plastered with stucco,

Copan, a Maya scientific center, as it looked in the Golden Age. Restoration drawing by Tatiana Proskouriakoff
PEABODY MUSEUM, HARVARD UNIVERSITY

*The ballcourt at Copan when it was in use. Restoration drawing by
Tatiana Proskouriakoff* PEABODY MUSEUM, HARVARD UNIVERSITY

The river that was—and is—the border of Copan, with the ruins rising beside it.
PEABODY MUSEUM, HARVARD UNIVERSITY

The "nunnery" at Uxmal, in Yucatan, where the Mayas' Golden Age flared into a brief rebirth, as it looks today. AMERICAN MUSEUM OF NATURAL HISTORY, NEW YORK

A recreation of the "nunnery" and its center court. It was probably a school for the youngsters of the nobility. Restoration drawing by Tatiana Proskouriakoff
PEABODY MUSEUM, HARVARD UNIVERSITY

was covered at measured intervals with carved stelae, in earth-toned red. Viewed from above, it must have looked somewhat like a chessboard, with each stele representing a king, knight or pawn of history.

After the Golden Age came to its end early in the tenth century A.D. a short-lived renaissance of the New Empire developed in what became known as the Puuc country, a stretch of soft plains and rolling hills in the Peninsula of Yucatan. Some lovely remains of the Puuc civilization can be seen at Uxmal in Mexico. The most beautiful building there is the "nunnery," so designated by the Spaniards. It was probably a school for the children of Maya nobles. It is arranged around a perfectly proportioned central court, the buildings on each side of the quadrangle covered with finely finished friezes of leaves and circles, garlands and houses, crosses, squares and curlicues, in muted tones of terra cotta, cream, and marbled gray. Some of the buildings in Uxmal have pillars that look like Corinthian columns. One edifice has the design we call a Greek key, reflecting under the close sun of the Tropic of Cancer lights and shadows in an ever-changing but always symmetrical pattern. Uxmal is hauntingly gentle and exquisite, and helps one to understand—and regret—the next period in the history of the Maya, the one the archeologists call the Mexican period.

At that time, from about 1000 A.D. on, the most powerful people in Mexico were the Toltecs, a rigidly organized martial people who founded the military orders and traditions that were later taken over by the Aztecs. The Toltecs, who held sway in Central Mexico, had long eyed with envy the splendid civilization of the Maya in the south. When the Maya came within the Toltecs' military reach by moving back north from the Central American isthmus into the Yucatan Peninsula, the temptation the Mayas' New Empire rep-

In their classic age, the Maya sculpted in the round. This stone figure dates from the classic period, about 600–900 A.D.
MUSEUM OF PRIMITIVE ART, NEW YORK

A chac mol at Chichen Itza. The face clearly shows the brutalizing Toltec influence.

resented was too great for the Toltecs to resist. By conquest or political pressure they brought one after another of the Mayan cities of the New Empire under Toltec overlordship.

Aiding the Toltecs in their military conquest was a new weapon, a mechanical spear-thrower, which gave Toltec arms a decisively longer range. It was a kind of crossbow that could send spears over distances many times greater than those the Maya could cover with their lances, which they threw by hand. The Toltecs also had better armor, a heavy cotton quilt that covered much of the face and most of the body. And they were better organized. But most important, the Toltecs cared about conquest. They wanted to conquer land, and they wanted to conquer people. They used captives as slaves and as sacrifices for their deities who, quite logically in so bloodthirsty a civilization, were thought to require human victims.

A characteristic Toltec figure, known as a *chac mol*, reflects this aspect of Toltec thought. A *chac mol's* face is round, primitive, bland. Its figure is shaped to make it possible for a human being to be stretched across it, arms and legs flung out, and the chest positioned so that a priest can get at it easily and, with a knife, cut deep quickly to lift out the still beating heart. This the Toltecs did, and offered the heart to their gods.

Human offerings to the rain gods were presented in a different fashion. Yucatan has large natural wells known as *cenotes*. When the Toltecs thought the rain gods needed appeasing, they drugged their sacrificial victims, usually young women or children, and after an intricate ritual dance, hurled them into a well. They were supposed to converse with the gods in the water and bring back news, if they could, about the gods' intentions. The victims were thrown into the *cenote* at dawn. At midday, priests went to the well

The famous cenote—sacrificial well—
at Chichen Itza.

Dredging the cenote has turned up a
large number of skulls and bones
of human sacrificial victims of the
Toltec period.

to see whether anyone had indeed returned with word from the water gods. If any victims did survive, they were honored as divine messengers. Few succeeded. *Cenotes* in the cities of Yucatan that fell under Toltec influence are strewn with skulls and bones in the depths of their swampy bottoms. Scattered among remains are jewels and pottery. These, too, were believed to be pleasing to the water gods.

A *cenote* at the mighty ruins of Chichen Itza, in Yucatan, has been partly dredged. Chichen Itza, a massive memento of the Toltec civilization, also has a *chac mol*, ready to receive sacrifice, and a ballcourt where the Maya ballgame *pok-to-pok* was played the Toltec way, with the heads of the players as stakes. A sculpted frieze on the ballcourt shows what happened when a game was over. Hulking Toltec temples and castles display the regimented methods and manners that made these Mexicans such successful warriors.

The Toltecs not only conquered the Maya, they also corrupted them. They introduced into Mayan religion their own bloodthirsty notions, requiring an ever-increasing quantity of human sacrifice. The Maya, too, had honored the gods by occasionally offering them blood, which they considered the substance of life, along with crops and jewels, incense and art. But the Maya blood-offering usually consisted of a man running a thorn over his tongue, or piercing his earlobe with a flint, to give to the gods a few drops of his own blood as a symbolic demonstration of devotion. The Toltecs killed and offered the living hearts of others—slaves and prisoners, the young, the defenseless. The Toltec passion for conquest sprang in part from their need for sacrificial victims.

Under Toltec influence, the practice spread among the Maya, and they too began to battle each other, with their cities now vying for power. What had been in the classic period a lissome net of communities held together by the silken strands of shared values, became under Toltec influence a rigid honeycomb of tribal cells, brittle and fragile. Indicatively, no Maya ceremonial center of the Golden Age had a wall around it, but everyone living or visiting was safe. After the Toltec conquest, every Maya city was surrounded by walls but remained vulnerable because of the corruption and distrust within.

When the Spaniards came early in the sixteenth century, internecine warfare and political rivalries among the Maya had reached a point that made the Mayas' complete subjugation by the conquistadors just about inevitable. The corrosive influence of the Mexican conquest had wormed its way through almost all of the Maya realm. Nearly everywhere in Maya territory, a tribe, a city, or a prince would collaborate with the Spaniards against a fellow-Mayan whom he considered a rival. The Spaniards used such rivalries skillfully and with complete ruthlessness. They divided, conquered, exterminated.

To the Spaniards, who at first knew nothing of the Mayan civilization, its duration and its glories, conquest of the Maya was a simple matter of geography.

In the Yucatan Peninsula they entrusted the campaign to conquistador Francisco de Montejo, who began it in 1527 but could not complete it himself and passed it on to his son, who fought the final battle in 1546. The conquest took two decades because the martial arts that the Yucatan Maya had learned from the Toltecs stiffened their physical, if not their moral, resistance.

In Honduras, conquistador Cristobal de Olid encountered little resistance.

In Guatemala there were a number of pitched battles, with conquistador Pedro de Alvarado leading the Spaniards. The most famous fight in the Alvarado campaign was with the Quiche, who authored the *Popol Vuh*. Spanish reports say that the Quiche had 50,000 warriors to meet Alvarado's 170 cavalrymen, 130 musketeers, 300 Mexican Indians, 120 horses and four pieces of artillery. The Quiche gave battle, led by their Prince Tecun Uman. The final encounter took place in the valley of the Olintepeque River, and the story goes that it was so wild and desperate a fight that, at the end of the day, the river ran red with blood. It has been called Blood River ever since.

Legend also has it that Prince Tecun Uman finally challenged Pedro de Alvarado to a personal duel, after killing Don Pedro's horse with a fighting stick. Alvarado mounted another horse and, sitting high in the saddle, ran his long lance through the throat of Tecun Uman, who was on foot looking up at the Spaniard. The battle took place in 1524 and effectively ended the resistance of the highland Maya.

In the lowlands, only one Maya city escaped the Spaniards until the end of the seventeenth century. The Itza, who had been part of the New Empire in the Yucatan Peninsula, fled south again after the Spaniards came to Mexico and settled on the islands of Lake Peten, deep in the jungle that had earlier sheltered Tikal. There, the Itza built their capital Tayasal, which the Spaniards did not discover until 1618, and did not conquer until 1697.

IV: BEFORE
THE COMING
OF THE MIGHTY MEN

BEFORE "THE COMING OF THE MIGHTY MEN"—THAT IS HOW THE Maya described the Spanish conquest—life in Mayadom was colorful, both literally and figuratively.

To begin with, an individual's social role among the Maya was indicated by body paint. Everyone daubed himself, often with intricate and artistic designs. Children were decorated with black paint; married people displayed their body color patterns in red. Warriors used both red and black, and lots of it, presumably to display the courage that animated them. Slaves, too, were generously covered with color, probably to make them easily recognizable. Their hues were black and white, which one imagines to have been as noticeable on the causeways of Tikal as the striped uniform of a prisoner

50

from Sing Sing would be in the streets of Manhattan. Priests and nobles were resplendent in sacred blue.

The Maya felt—as men and women have throughout history—that they had to improve on nature to achieve beauty. The Maya's natural build is short and stocky, with a rather broad head, full face and delicate hands and feet. The classic Maya did not like their square heads and round faces. They thought that an elegant head should be long and thin. To achieve this look, mothers who cared about appearance put the heads of their children, when the bones of the skull were still soft and malleable, between two wooden boards, applying gentle but steady pressure. This produced a back-sloping forehead that indeed created an impression of length. It also resulted in what was in effect a pointed head, an impression the Maya emphasized further by enlarging their noses with putty or by attaching weighty jewelry to the nostrils thus assuring the noses' prominence and droop. Earlobes were equally distended by heavy ornaments. The Maya also thought eyes that were turned inward toward each other bespoke a meditative nature, and were therefore spiritual and appealing. To induce this spiritual look, Maya mothers invented yet another device which they used to beautify their children at an early age. It consisted of a bead fixed to a thong around a baby's forehead. The bead, or a ball of pitch, swung with the slightest motion of child or wind, and the baby's eyes involuntarily followed the glittering object. The result was a permanently cross-eyed look.

The combination of sloping forehead and prominent nose, distended earlobes and pupils of the eye turned toward each other, made the chin appear recessive. The classic Maya thought that this was a noble appearance and pleasing to the gods. It did create an air of concentrated contemplation.

Left, a Maya face in its natural state. This is how the Maya looked—and look now—when their features were not distorted to meet the Maya notion of beauty. This stone head is from Copan.

<small>AMERICAN MUSEUM OF NATURAL HISTORY, NEW YORK (LEFT)</small>

Right, this is what the classic Maya would have considered a beautiful face: sloping forehead, putty-enlarged nose, big pierced ear lobes, eyes turned inward for a contained, meditative look. This head is from Palenque.

<small>INSTITUTO NACIONAL DE ANTROPOLOGIA E HISTORIA, MEXICO (RIGHT)</small>

To counterbalance this ascetic inwardness, the Maya were extravagant in their facial decoration. They hung themselves like Christmas trees, with ornaments dangling from their nostrils, earlobes, and lips. If they were of the upper classes, they also tattooed their cheeks.

A Maya ruler in the classic age was covered in splendor from the tip of his toe to way above the top of his head. On his head, he wore a panache that rose as high as three feet, with feathers that swept in his wake for as much as four feet. The feathers had the iridescent colors of the quetzal bird, a deep blue-green, flecked with brilliant red and glowing yellow. The body was covered by a breechclout of fine cotton, heavily embroidered and decorated with feathers; a vest of jaguar pelt covered the chest. Alternatively, the breechclout was made of jaguar hide, with the skin's markings carefully preserved. A flowing mantle, encrusted with jewels or plumes, hung from the shoulders. Feet were encased in tooled sandals with heel guards of jaguar hide.

Every available part of the body around which jewelry could be hung, and from which decoration could be draped, was embellished with jade, coral, shell, copper and gold. These substances were carved into earplugs and nose rings, and shaped into beads the size of plums to hang from the neck or to serve as bracelets and anklets. They were fashioned into beltbuckles and pendants. To make certain that no area of the body was left untouched by art, teeth were filed and inlaid with shell or glittering pieces of pyrite. Polished pyrite, in reflecting disks, was affixed to the hair.

The Maya idea of splendor called for repeating the colors of the rainbow in a man's costume. Some colors had symbolic meaning as well. Red, for example, was the color of blood and, therefore, of

*A Maya ruler was covered in splendor from head to foot,
like the* halach uinic *shown seated here. This is a rubbing
from a stone lintel in Bonampak.*

A Maya woman, in her chemise, wearing earrings, a large
necklace and bracelets. This seated figure is from the area
near the island of Jaina, Mexico.

MUSEUM OF PRIMITIVE ART, NEW YORK

life. Yellow represented the ripe corn and by implication all nourishment. Black, the color of obsidian, represented weapons and death. Green, the color of the quetzal bird's feathers and also the young shoots of corn, stood for all that was noble, growing and hopeful. Blue, the color of the sky, was sacred.

For everyday wear, and for the Maya who worked in the fields or forests, dress was a much less complicated affair. At its simplest, it consisted of an oblong sheet of cotton that was used as a cover at night and, wrapped around the body, served as a mantle during the day. A cotton breechclout went with it, and simple, thonged sandals.

Women's dress consisted primarily of a chemise, made by sewing together a length of cotton, then cutting one hole into it for the neck, and two for the arms. Like the breechclout, the chemise could vary from one of unadorned cotton to one profusely decorated with embroidery, brocade, or feathers. Working women who had to move around a great deal wore nothing but this chemise, which came to just above the knee. Ladies whose status in life required less physical mobility wore beneath their chemises a cotton skirt that reached to the ankles. All women carried stoles, which could be wrapped around shoulder and throat for protection, or draped across the hair and part of the face for modesty or style.

Women did not wear sandals. They walked barefoot, possibly to display their feet, which were small and graceful. Maya women also had a lovely way of displaying their hands. They joined them in front, clasping a bouquet of fragrant flowers, which they brought up to their bejewelled noses every so often to inhale the perfume of the petals, showing off their elegant fingers at the same time.

Maya women used other perfume as well, beads of sweet-smelling resins which they dabbed on their foreheads.

A Maya man, wearing only the most basic everyday garment: a breechclout. (From Jaina, Mexico)
MUSEUM OF PRIMITIVE ART, NEW YORK

A Maya woman, with her child and dog, wearing a chemise starting at the waist. This was rare. Most chemises covered the entire body. (From Chiapas, Mexico)
UNIVERSITY MUSEUM, UNIVERSITY OF PENNSYLVANIA

Both men and women, of whatever occupation or social class, wore their hair long. Men let it fall straight down to the shoulder, or pulled it together into a ponytail, with a tonsure cut at the crown and bangs reaching to the eye. Women either plaited their hair into braids, or swept it up into elaborate hairdos resembling beehives, and curled it into masses of ringlets. Little girls usually had their hair twisted into four short pigtails standing up like horns in the front and back of the head. As a general rule, women wore less jewelry than men.

Maya manners seem to have been exquisite. This was not the result of inculcated artifice, but a natural expression of alert and sensitive consideration for others which the Maya were taught from infancy.

In a Maya household, children were both loved and respected by their elders, and the relationship was reciprocal. Children were treated as adults, in the sense that they were taken seriously as complete, individual personalities, capable of assuming responsibilities and making decisions within their competence. They were given responsibilities as soon as they were physically able to handle them. For boys, this meant accompanying their fathers to the fields, the woods, the streams, as soon as they could be of help in the sowing, planting and harvesting, the hunting, trapping and fishing. In the winter months, boys, as soon as they could stay awake long enough, joined their fathers around the glowing embers or under the bright stars, to flake flints for knives and spears, make rope for sandals, arrows and bags, or carve obsidian for tools or offerings.

Girls ground corn and baked corn patties, cured meat and cooked vegetables, raised animals and cultivated fruit trees, spun and wove as soon as their hands were large enough to hold the implements.

The Maya loved personal decoration.
This is an ornament made of shell.
MUSEUM OF PRIMITIVE ART, NEW YORK

A pottery whistle in the shape of a
man wearing a tassled, embroidered
breechclout, necklace, earrings and
feather headdress, and carrying a
banner. (From Campeche, Mexico)
UNIVERSITY MUSEUM,
UNIVERSITY OF PENNSYLVANIA

They learned by watching their mothers, as the boys learned their crafts by emulating their fathers. In the process, the children acquired respect for the knowledge of their elders, while the parents were proud and delighted to watch the growing skills of their offspring.

Obedience was rarely a problem. It followed naturally from respect and from the love children felt for their parents with whom they spent so much of their time, and who helped them in everything that was important in their lives. Parents in turn cared deeply about their children. Their feeling of responsibility and concern was ever-present, and constituted an emulation of the way parents assumed the gods felt about them.

A prayer that has survived from the classic times among an isolated group of Maya known as the Lancandon, who were never converted to Christianity, expresses this relationship. The prayer is offered by a father for his son who is ill. The father, addressing the Heart of Heaven says:

Guard my son, my father. Cause any evil to cease. Cause the fever to cease. Do not allow evil to trample him underfoot. Do not allow a snake to bite my son. Do not permit my son's death when he is at play. When he is grown up, he will give you an offering of corn mush. When he is grown up, he will give you an offering of corn cakes. When he is grown, he will give you an offering of bark strips. When he is grown up, he will remember you.

Relationships between men and women, another barometer of the degree to which a civilization has evolved, also seem to have achieved a high level of harmony. They were based on a respect for women that was extraordinary for its time. It can be seen graphically on the murals of Bonampak, where ladies of the court observe the rituals and festivals depicted, looking very self-assured. It can also be seen in Copan, where a stele in the main court shows a woman *halach uinic*, her expression meditative and wise, but clearly commanding. She wears a skirt instead of a breechclout, but it is made of jaguar skin, symbolizing power. The face is softer and rounder than the visages of the male rulers with whom she now shares the court, but she carries her serpent scepter, sign of the highest temporal authority, with complete, and very calm, conviction.

More indicative still of the life women led in Mayadom is a modeled head in the museum of Santa Rosa de Copan, near the ruins. The head portrays a Maya "Mrs. John Doe." She has none of the trappings of special status. Her hair is swept up into a simple bun; her nose is aquiline as required by the Maya notions of beauty; her eyes are almond-shaped. She looks handsome, self-possessed, and at peace.

A precise division of labor existed between men and women, and their respective roles were closely defined. Generally, men handled chores outside the home—they cultivated the fields, hunted, fished, traded, traveled the roads and the seas, built the temples, and tracked the stars—while women did the work in the house and its environs. Those environs reached out quite far, however, and included a considerable variety of activities. Women, in their gardens, raised such luxury crops as avocado bushes, vanilla trees, peppers and the *achiote*, which produced an important red pigment used as a dye. Women also kept animals in their backyards. These included monkeys, which were acquired for fun as well as food, ducks that were raised for their feathers, and bees that were kept for the honey that was the major ingredient in the famous honeyfire of festive occasions. Women went to market to sell some of these home-grown luxuries, and traded them for such esoteric items as topaz nose rings and pyrite mirror disks for their men, or obsidian knive blades, flint needles, and bone awls for themselves. Women did all the spinning and weaving and were responsible as well for the embroidery of breechclouts and the manufacture of feather capes, mantles and head-dresses. Women also made and decorated pottery for domestic and ceremonial use. Only the symbolic figures of deities were shaped by men, sculptors who worked in temple apartments.

If some quirk of the seasons, such as early rains or a particularly strong sun, called for an all-out effort in the fields, women sometimes joined their men to get the work done in time. Maya women did not lead a sheltered existence. Characteristically, when the men had im-bibed honeyfire for spiritual or social reasons to the point where their motor control could no longer be depended upon, women got them home safely, propping them up on the way, or even carrying them on their backs if that was necessary. It occasionally was.

Women were considered partners in life—precious partners. All important ceremonies defining or celebrating the individual's relation-ship to life involved women along with men. This began with the very first such ceremony, the *hetzmek*, which was held when a baby girl was three months old or a baby boy four months old. It consisted of the child being carried around the room nine times astride the hip of the godfather if it was a boy, the godmother if it was a girl. Each time the circle was completed, an object that was either a miniature version or a symbol of the tools the baby would use during its life, was placed into the baby's hand. For a girl, the objects included a spindle or a pestle to crush corn; for a boy, a digging stick or a hunting sling and pellet.

The ceremony was held three months after a girl's birth, because the symbol of a Maya woman's life was the hearth consisting of three stones. The four-month period chosen for a boy's *hetzmek* was symbolic of his major concern, the corn field, with its four corners.

Later in each Maya child's life came the *emku*, the ritual initiation into adult life, not very different in attitude and meaning from Christian communion. Girls went through this ceremony at age twelve, boys at fourteen. The ritual was the same for both, and mothers as well as fathers attended it.

Marriage in Maya society was regarded as a family partnership. Parents kept an eye out for the kind of girl they wanted for their son, and when they had found her, hired a marriage maker to sound out the prospective in-laws and make the required arrangements. It was considered mean-spirited for families to negotiate directly. Arrangements involved a dowry, paid by the groom's father to the girl's parents. The groom's father also defrayed the cost of marriage festivities, and the groom's mother wove the special wedding garments for the couple. After marriage, the new husband went to the family compound of his wife and worked for his father-in-law for a number of years.

The marriage ceremony itself was simple. A priest came to the house of the groom's father, who presented the couple. The priest then read the arrangements that had been worked out by the marriage maker and, there being no argument, blessed the bride and groom who knelt before him. There were no pledges of troth. The groom demonstrated his loyalty by the work he did for his father-in-law. The bride showed her devotion by providing her husband with food. If either one failed to perform these duties, such neglect was grounds for divorce. Divorce was very simple indeed. It consisted of the aggrieved party returning to his or her parents.

Despite their treasured position, or perhaps because of it, women maintained manners of modesty. They did not eat with their husbands, fathers and sons, but served the men first and took their own meals afterwards. This was largely a matter of practical necessity, since it is difficult even today, and was not possible then, to serve graciously and eat a meal at the same time.

The Maya applied a sensible graciousness to most of their social relationships. They were, for instance, very hospitable, but guarded their privacy at the same time. A visitor was always welcome, and this included strangers. Every caller was offered food and drink and, if the household was not prepared for a guest, the home's mistress would borrow what she needed from a neighbor. Guests rarely departed without being given a present, and such presents could range from the ceramic cup in which they had been served their beverage to a length of feather-embroidered cotton. While hospitality was thus generously practiced, privacy went with it. Even the simplest Maya home had a string of bells at the side of the doorway, which was often open. Visitors would make their presence known by touching the bells. In well-equipped households, the doorway had a grass or cotton mat strung across it, and was flanked by bells. In addition to tinkling pleasantly and alerting the household to guests, the bells also served to carry the sound beyond the house to the backyard, where the ladies might be weaving or making pottery, and to the garden where they might be at work watering and pruning their trees, or feeding their animals.

Backyards tended to be sizable and usually contained two installations characteristic of Maya life: the steambath and the storage bin. The steambath consisted of two chambers dug into the ground, connected by an opening in the wall. One chamber had a hollow that could be filled with water. The water was warmed by putting hot stones into the hollow. The hissing stones also made the steam that escaped into the second chamber through the opening in the wall.

The Maya first took a bath, then a steam bath, a cleansing process that had ritual meaning for them as well as hygienic purpose. They washed their hands and mouth before each meal, and took a bath each dawn before going off into the fields or out to hunt, and again as dusk before eating the main meal of the day. When the Spaniards first observed these Maya habits, they came to the conclusion that the Mayas' coloring, which ranges from a creamy cacao to a burnished copper, was the result of all this washing and steaming. The Spaniards believed that all of these daily abolutions rubbed the white pigment off the skin.

Domestic utensils in Maya households were often beautiful as well as practical. All these are from Copan. They are, left to right, a jar, a vase, another jar.
CARNEGIE INSTITUTE, WASHINGTON, D.C.

The storage bin, usually located in the backyard corner opposite the steambath, was called a *chultun* and it, too, was dug into the earth. A *chultun* could be anything from a limestone-lined hole in the ground to a whole series of chambers lined with plaster, starting with a bell-shaped antechamber covered with a round limestone lid. In Tikal, archeologists have found *chultuns* with as many as nine storage chambers and have come to the conclusion that their size depended on the wealth of the families that built them. *Chultuns* were used to store ears of corn, tubers, preserved squashes and fruit, and probably dried and salted meats.

To bring in the crops and meats that filled these larders, Maya men worked together in teams. They went out to the fields in groups of twenty, tilling each man's plot in turn. They hunted and fished in groups, and pooled their catch. After taking off the portions due their spiritual and temporal rulers, they divided the rest according to need, which was determined by the size of each man's family.

They built together as well. When a new house was needed for a just-married couple, or because a dwelling had burned down or been blown over by a storm, or was in need of renewal, all the men in the compound (villages were usually organized into compounds, with several houses built around a common front yard) set out for the forest to collect the required materials. The next day, they started on the house and with everyone pitching in, beginning at dawn, the dwelling was usually finished by dusk.

Farmers' houses were simple structures, the walls made of wood or sun-baked earth. In the lowlands the homes were roofed with a thatch of palm leaves or the rain-resistant webbing of other jungle trees; in the highlands with straw and dried grasses. Some of the houses were oblong, some square, some circular. Paths ran from the village compounds to the major, raised causeways that led to the city, where the market was held and religious ceremonies took place. Usually, the more important a family was, the closer it lived to the heart of town.

The dark aspect of social relations—crime—was treated in a sensible, considerate manner. The Maya did not absolutely prohibit a person touching another's property. A rule allowed anyone who was hungry to go to the field—anyone's field—and help himself to two ears of corn. This was considered enough to assuage hunger. If a man took more, however, he was considered a thief and the Maya

*Home furnishings, from Copan. They
are, top to bottom, two views of a
tripod jar in which hot food was
served, and a decorated vase.*

did not approve of stealing. Punishment was severe but logical. It required the thief to work off the debt he owed to the person from whom he had stolen, usually with double or triple indemnity. This done, the thief was held to have paid his debt to society and nothing more was made of it. If a thief turned out to be a repeat offender, he was chased out of the village and not allowed to return.

Homicide was rare, and punishable by death. The Maya made no distinction between murder and manslaughter. They saw the issue from the victim's point of view. As far as they were concerned, the victim was dead and only one punishment fitted that crime.

A piece of Maya writing describes social relationships among the classic Maya by contrasting them with what happened after the Spaniards came. In one mind-wrenching paragraph, it tells of the harmony the Maya had created and the chaos the conquistadors brought. The description comes from the Book of Chilam Balam of Chumayel, which was written in Latin letters, but in a Maya language, two generations after the conquest.

It reads:

Before the coming of the mighty men and Spaniards, there was no robbery by violence, there was no greed and striking down one's fellow man in his blood, at the cost of the poor man, at the expense of the food of each and everyone.

It [the coming of the Spaniards] was the beginning of tribute, the beginning of church dues, the beginning of strife with purse snatching, the beginning of strife with guns, the beginning of strife by trampling of people, the beginning of robbery with violence, the beginning of debts enforced by false testimony, the beginning of individual strife, a beginning of vexation.

V: RULERS, JUDGES, AND CAPTAINS

THERE SEEMS TO HAVE BEEN A MINIMUM OF "VEXATION," THAT is, social friction, among the Maya during the 600 years of their Golden Age. Classic Maya society was meticulously organized. It had an elaborately structured hierarchy which was, however, neither rigid nor totalitarian. Social mobility was possible, and the government was responsive to the people, with channels of communication carefully maintained with the grassroots or, more accurately, the corn shoots and the people who cultivated them. As a result, rulers were, with very few exceptions, popular in Webster's triple sense of that word: they were "carried on by, or intended for, people generally; liked by many people; having many friends."

Maya society was also enjoyable. While social roles and community functions were closely defined for every man, woman and child in Mayadom, obligations were accompanied by celebrations to prevent these duties from becoming dull or onerous. The feeling of awe and wonder that permeated the intensely religious civilization of the Maya was given fulfillment in eye- and mind-dazzling ritual, and exhilarating worship provided release.

At the top of the Mayan hierarchy stood the *halach uinic*, the "true man," who combined in himself three facets of knowledge and action. For each of these he had a scepter, symbol of his authority. As temporal ruler, chief administrator of his city state and its environs, he carried a scepter representing an idealized and highly stylized version of Maya man at his most complete. It had an elaborate feathered top, standing for the plumage of the quetzal, symbol of the wings of man's imagination and spirit. The scepter's lower half displayed the head of a serpent, symbol of fertility and material creation.

The second scepter of the *halach uinic* represented his religious authority. It was a large double-headed ceremonial bar, which was carried horizontally across the chest. Its two heads were a typical Maya amalgam of man, serpent and jaguar, the jaguar in this instance serving as an image of energy. The bar was completely symmetrical, with the two heads standing for the complexities of human life that can, however, be brought into harmony by balance and moderation.

His third scepter was a martial one, representing the ruler as the highest military personage of the state, in the same way that the President of the United States is commander in chief of the armed forces. The martial scepter was a finely wrought, stylized weapon:

The two scepters of the halach uinic:
Left, the double-headed bar, symbol of
religious authority. Right, stylized feathers
and an animal head, symbol of temporal
authority.
UNIVERSITY MUSEUM,
UNIVERSITY OF PENNSYLVANIA (LEFT)
MUSEUM OF PRIMITIVE ART, NEW YORK (RIGHT)

*A halach uinic conferring with his counselors. This is a
portion of the murals in the temple at Bonampak.*
CARNEGIE INSTITUTE, WASHINGTON, D.C.

either a long, elegantly shaped spear with a fine obsidian blade; or a throwing stick, which was a kind of boomerang devised by the Maya early in the classical age; or a simple club, not unlike the one Neanderthal man used in Europe to hunt bison and bear.

In his capacity as civil ruler, the *halach uinic* governed with the advice of high priests and a collection of counselors. Some of the counselors were assigned specific functions and constituted a cabinet. Their various posts had highly descriptive designations. The Treasury Secretary was "Lord of the Bracelets"; the Secretary of State, who received foreign ambassadors and their tribute, was "Lord of Those Who Give"; the Secretary of the Interior was "Grand Master of the Feasts." Every *halach uinic* also had one cabinet member for whom, unfortunately, no counterpart exists in our political system: "The Master of the Hall of Council and of the Game of Ball." In contemporary terms this would be a cabinet officer combining the functions of chief of the National Security Council with those of baseball commissioner.

Most cabinet members were scions of the royal family, although state functionaries at any level could be elected, and sometimes were.

The advisory team of the *halach uinic* also included a group of counselors known as the *ah-kulekob*, who were chosen for special talents or expertise. Their jobs seem to have been comparable to those of special White House assistants.

The setting for policy-making was one of restrained splendor. Palaces were sizable, with many rooms, but very simply constructed. They consisted of a long row of chambers of handsome proportions but comparatively small and dark. Arched doorways, covered with feather curtains, were the only source of light. This produced a contained, meditative effect within the council rooms.

The *halach uinic* sat on a throne placed on a reed mat, wearing a full set of jewels and his tall, feathered crown. The throne was surmounted by four canopies of feathers. Similar feather canopies, but smaller and fewer in number, swayed over the mats of the other lords in attendance. Feather canopies were an insignia of rank, while feather fans served as passports, their size and color indicating the status and origin of the bearer. Ambassadors presented their credentials by extending their fans to the *halach uinic*.

Decisions made in council sessions affected foreign as well as domestic policy, including taxation. Policies were communicated to the people by relays of town criers who spread the word to every corner of the city-state, shaking rattles to draw attention to their messages.

The city-states had subsidiary towns or villages, roughly comparable to our suburbs, and these were governed by provincial administrators called *batabs*. As a rule, *batabs* were appointed to their posts by the *halach uinic* and were members of the nobility through the maternal line. They did, however, have to pass an examination which was also open to men who were not of the nobility. It seems to have been a system akin to the Chinese mandarin establishment. *Batabs* had civil and military functions, although in the second capacity they were assisted, in fact guided, by an elected officer, the *nacom*.

In his civilian capacity, the *batab* duplicated the *halach uinic* at the local level. He presided over the town or village council, saw to it that temples were properly maintained, houses kept in good repair, streets swept, and fields cultivated. He was counseled by priests who kept the sacred and temporal calendars and who also advised the *batab* on the proper times for religious festivals and the appropriate seasons for the clearing, sowing, planting and harvesting of the fields.

The *batab* also served as judge, ruling on civil and criminal cases. When he thought a legal matter to be beyond his comprehension or jurisdiction, he asked for and received advice from the *halach uinic*. As tax collector, the *batab* was responsible for gathering the tribute due the *halach uinic* and his retinue.

The *batab* himself was supported by tribute from his local citizens. Taxes were paid in kind, on a graduated scale, with the rich paying more than the poor. There is some evidence that a special section of cities, towns and villages was set aside to provide welfare services to the maimed and old who could no longer look after themselves. The tax they owed the *halach uinic* was paid by the *batab* out of his own resources.

Tax payments consisted of crops from the farmer, game from the hunter, sea food from the fisherman. A merchant paid his tribute in goods, ranging from strings of copper bells to lengths of cotton, obsidian blades and jade beads to flaked flint, shells, stingrays, coral, and gold ornaments. Salt and *pom*, the tree resin used for incense, honey and wax, and above all cacao beans, which were the closest equivalent the Maya had to a currency, were acceptable as tax payments. The *halach uinic's* seneschal resold what was not needed in the royal or priestly households to merchant wholesalers, who funneled the surplus goods into the public retail markets, collecting currency in return. To the *halach uinic* the advantage of currency over goods was mainly that it was easier to store, and the Lord of the Bracelets was probably in charge of all such transactions.

At the local level, *batabs* had their own staffs and counselors to assist them in governing towns or village complexes. Local counselors were called *cuch cabob*, and apparently fulfilled a function similar to that of borough presidents in a city like New York, with the *batab* equivalent to the mayor. They represented sections of the town, had a vote in city government, and the *batab* had to have their concurrence on all important policy decisions. In executing policy, the *batab* was assisted by the *kulekob*, who accompanied the *batab* on his official rounds and saw to it that policies were translated into action effectively and quickly. It seems to have been an efficient, smoothly working system. Vestiges of it still exist in the self-contained Maya communities of today's Guatemala, where local government functions with calm competence under social arrangements that differ little from Maya government in the classic age.

The reason for its success now and then is probably the combination of organization and responsiveness, a responsiveness attuned not only to the public will, but to the more subtle reality of public desire. This, too, was institutionalized. Rulers were kept in daily touch with the thoughts and feelings of their people through another specialized set of officials, the *holpopob*. Literally translated, *holpopob* means those who sit at the head of the mat. The mat was a highly symbolic concept to the Maya, representing communication: between man and his fellow; man and his ruler; man and his gods.

The *holpopob*, sitting at the head of the community's mat, listened to the voice of the people. If a citizen wanted to convey a request or a question to his *batab*, to express a desire or a doubt, he conveyed his thoughts and sentiments to the *holpopob*. The *holpopob* probably used his own judgment to decide which of these communications should be passed on to the *batab*. The man sitting at the head of the mat had to see to it that the governor was not beset by trivial or unreasonable bother, and make certain at the same time that people were afforded the opportunity to tell the *batab* what was on their minds.

The *holpopob* had a pretty good idea of just what was on people's minds even before individuals came to tell him. *Holpopobs* were the "masters," that is, the chairmen, of the Mayan equivalent of town hall meetings. Each Maya town and village had a special house in which the men of the community discussed public issues, and rehearsed dances for festivals. Being Mayans, they considered the two functions equally important. The *holpopob* presided over the debating sessions, and supervised the dance rehearsals. He was also the chief singer at ritual performances, and the musical instruments of the town were in his charge. He was clearly a man of many parts and connections—and *batabs* made certain that they were in close and constant touch with the *holpopobs* of every community under their jurisdiction.

Tightly structured and alertly responsive, the system required little enforcement. However, each community did have a handful of constables, known as *tupiles*. These men constituted the bottom rung of the governing structure, and the ambition of the average Mayan was to have nothing to do with a *tupil*. In the few Maya communities that survive, this ambition still exists.

In classical times, justice was administered in what is probably one of the most sophisticated and humane methods yet devised. The judge's task was to make the litigants see each other's point of view, and have both parties agree to his ruling. Maya judges issued consent decrees, in both the literal and comprehensive meanings of that term.

Commercial relations among the Maya were as carefully and effectively ordered as were political affairs. The Maya traded widely, their merchants traveling by causeway and canoe from coast to coast across the isthmus and lengthwise through the continent for thousands of miles. Mayan markets were colorful places. Stalls of black and purple obsidian glittered alongside shimmering beads of jade in many shades of green; the salt merchants lined up in their section of the market, facing the sellers of gold, coral, and shells. Corn and cotton, powdered lime and flint blades, dried fowl and salted fish, bowls and platters of decorated ceramic, carved and painted flutes and figurines, seals and stamps, tooled sandals and feathered breechclouts, jaguar capes and shell nose rings, each had a designated row in the precisely planned public market.

Markets were laid out in squares or large rectangles, the outer area consisting of pillared arcades, roofed to provide protection against the sun. The more important merchants had their stalls in these arcades. The inner part of the market was open to the sky and sellers sat on mats, with their merchandise piled up before them. Each seller dealt in one kind of merchandise only, in the special section assigned to his wares. There was a section for jewelry and a section for foods, a section for tools and a section for housewares, a section for clothes and a section for building materials. The remains of a Mayan market, its tall, even pillars still evoking an attractive sense of order, can be seen at Chichen Itza. The village markets held today in the Mayan communities of Guatemala follow a similar pattern.

The Maya of the classic age had no money, in the sense of bills or coins. Their main currency was cacao, a delicious thought. As one archeologist put it, "they were on the chocolate standard." They also used chains of copper bells, collections of shells, or lengths of cotton as currency. The beans were equivalents of our nickels and dimes, the shells were quarters and half dollars, the copper bells were silver dollars, and the lengths of cotton served as dollar bills.

There existed apparently the occasional small crook who would

The inner arcades of a Maya market at Chichen Itza.

Another recreation of the market at Chichen Itza, where
the original pillars still stand. Both are restoration drawings
by Tatiana Proskouriakoff

peel cacao beans, take out the chocolate and fill the skins with sand. Since cacao beans usually were exchanged in small sacks, a buyer or seller who did not look at his change carefully could be fooled this way.

To prevent such cheating, and make certain that no serious disputes arose, an overseer attended each market session. If any differences emerged between trading partners that could not be settled, the problem was brought to the overseer. He solved it, following the method used by judges in civil and criminal cases. His consent decrees were based on the provisions of a commercial code which, of course, he had mastered in detail. His presence seems to have been largely preventative. The Maya cherished honesty; commercial contracts were made without documents of any kind. Nothing was written, signed, or mortgaged. A transaction was legalized by the two parties sharing a cup of honeyfire before witnesses.

Mayan books, as far as we know, never concerned themselves with goods, trade, tribute or accounting of any kind. In contrast, the Inca, who had no written language, did have the *quipu*, a sort of abacus made of knotted strings, with which they kept accounts of taxes and tributes, populations, and the services the people owed their ruler. And the Aztecs, who had written records, devoted a number of them to commercial matters.

Like all human societies before and after them, the Maya sometimes became embroiled in war. It did not happen frequently, by the standards of their day, and skirmishes were usually brief, limited, and ritualized.

Military planning was undertaken jointly by the *batab* and his military advisor the *nacom*. The *nacom* was elected for a three-year period, and lived those years with the combination of rigor and

*A Maya warrior in full uniform. This pottery whistle was
found near Chama, in Guatemala.*

Battle scenes, from the temple murals at Bonampak.
CARNEGIE INSTITUTE, WASHINGTON, D.C.

adulation, danger and glory that seems to be the lot of military leaders everywhere. While in office, the *nacom* had to be continent. He lived apart from his wife and family if he was married and was not allowed to eat red meat, use spices, or drink honeyfire.

On the other hand, a conquistador observer reports, "they held him in great veneration . . . they bore him in great pomp, perfuming him as if he were an idol, to the temple where they seated him and burned incense to him."

This ceremony was celebrated during the month of Pax, which was dedicated to Ek Chua, a god who doubled as the deity of war and the patron of merchants. He was usually pictured with narrowed eyes and a deeply drooping upper lip. He was painted black. In his capacity as the god of trade he held in his hands a bundle of goods. As god of war, he clasped a spear.

When the Maya actually went to war, the *nacom* and a statue of Ek Chua were carried to the battlefield in palanquins. The fighting seems to have been very much like a medieval joust, with a religious dimension added. Before the battle began, the opposing forces saluted each other, complimented each other on their bravery, then jointly performed an act of obeisance to the god of war. Thereafter, the battle was started, lasting usually until dusk or until a *nacom* was wounded or killed.

Maya officers used feathers instead of metal to designate their rank, and could therefore be recognized easily. This was particularly true of the *nacom*, who had feathers on his shield, his arms, his head. Since killing him was tantamount to snatching victory, he must have been a popular as well as a highly visible target.

The Maya not only brought their war god along but had women accompany them as well, to carry and prepare their food. The army was a combination of regular forces, each having its own captain and a distinguishing tall banner. Citizen soldiers were recruited as the need arose. The citizen-recruits seem not to have been very dependable fighting men. They responded to recruitment only in the winter season, between the time the harvest had been brought in and the preparation of the fields began in the spring. Whenever the recruits felt that families or fields, hunting or fishing grounds needed them, they had a tendency to melt away in the night.

Mayan soldiers fought mainly with spears, clubs, their own brand of boomerang and, in close combat, with broad flint knives. They had shields for defense, initially made of rushes, but later of hide. After their encounter with the Toltecs, the Maya apparently copied from the Mexicans their armor, a thick cotton quilt that had been soaked in brine to stiffen the cloth, which protected most of the torso.

The Mayan arsenal contained two weapons unreported to date in any other civilization. One of these, designed for close-up fighting, was a three-pronged claw knife, fashioned from a large, hard shell. A warrior could literally tear his enemy to pieces with this device. The other was a long-range weapon, reflecting the nastier aspects of Mayan ingenuity. It was a wasp bomb, a swarm of angry wasps with mean stings encased in a brittle gourd. When the gourd hit anything at all, preferably of course the body or face of an enemy soldier, it would break open to release its furious, waspish contents. Since both the gourds and the insects were lightweight, a wasp bomb could be hurled from quite a distance. None of the conquistadors who captured Maya lands ever reported being struck by a wasp bomb. They would probably have considered it an indignity to be felled by such a device. Nevertheless, it must have been an effective weapon.

VI: THE SACRED BALLGAME

TWIN HIERARCHIES GOVERNED MAYAN LIFE DURING THE CLASSIC
age. Matching in size and complexity the pyramid of civil authorities
was the pyramid of ecclesiastic authorities, the hierarchy of priests
whose offices and functions touched Mayan life at every point.

Priests were the guardians as well as the carriers of the main
strains of Maya civilization. They served as consultants to the
halach uinic and to the *batabs* in all major political decisions. No
Mayan army would depart for battle without the blessing of a
priest, no artist would either begin a work, or consider it finished,
unless it had received consecration. Priests served as instructors for
the sons of Maya nobles in all branches of knowledge that the Maya
cared about: astronomy, calendrics, mathematics, as well as as-

trology, theology and ethics. They taught princely families in the cities, and the sons—perhaps also the daughters—of ruling families in the towns and villages. Priests themselves were engaged in all the activities that challenged the Maya mind: the exploration of the planets, the calculation of time, the composition of books. And it was the priest, of course, who determined the seasons of the Maya working man. He told the farmer when to sow, plant and harvest; the hunter when to look for game; the merchant when to set out on a journey by land or by sea.

The important events of every Mayan's personal life had priests in attendance. A priest cast the new-born child's horoscope to determine its name and profession. Priests instructed children at their initiation ceremonies. A priest pronounced a man and woman husband and wife, and said the prayer of the dead when a Mayan was laid to final rest.

There were as many ranks and special functions in the ecclesiastical hierarchy as there were among the secular lords. At the top of the priestly pyramid stood the high priest, the *ahuacan*. The word means "the Lord Serpent." His position was hereditary, or so early Spanish historians report, and theirs is the only evidence we have to date. The most famous of these Spanish chroniclers of Maya ways was a priest, Bishop Diego de Landa, who encountered and observed the Maya during the first three decades of the conquest. It was an ambivalent encounter. The bishop was sufficiently hemmed in by the religious prejudices of his time to consider the Maya idolatrous heathens whose gods and books were works of the devil. He set out to destroy both and was unfortunately successful. But with all his medieval bias, the bishop could not help but be fascinated by the many-splendored civilization he saw, and his reluctant admiration seeps through the careful accounts he kept of the years in which the Maya of Yucatan were subjects of his diocese.

From Bishop Landa we learn that "he [the *ahuacan*] was very much respected by the lords . . . who, besides offerings, made him presents, and all the priests of the town brought contributions to him. . . . In him was the key of their learning and it was to these matters that they [the high priests] mostly dedicated themselves. And they gave advice to the lords and replied to their questions."

Impressed, and possibly envious, Bishop Landa continues his description:

They seldom dealt with matters pertaining to sacrifices except at the time of the principal feasts, or very important matters of business. They provided priests for the towns where they were needed, examining them in the sciences and ceremonies, and committed to them the duties of their office, and how to set a good example to people, and provided them with books and sent them forth. And they employed themselves in the duties of the temples and in teaching their sciences as well as writing books about them.

The sciences which they taught were the computation of the years, months, and days, the festivals and ceremonies, the administration of the sacraments, the fateful days and seasons, their methods of divination and their prophecies, events and the cures for diseases, and their history and how to read and write with their letters and characters and to make drawings which illustrate the meaning of the writings.

Immediately below the high priest ranked the *chilan*, whose duty it was to find out what the gods had in mind, and to convey divine intentions and desires to the people. The word *chilan* means messenger, and these priests were thought to be messengers who carried the gods' word to man. They were the Mayan counterpart of angels, except that they existed in the flesh. *Chilanes* were treated with great respect, and whenever a *chilan* stepped down from his temple sanctuary, the people would hoist him on their shoulders and carry him through the streets.

The people did not feel as appreciative of another priestly group: the clergymen who carried out the vital but despised job of opening the victim's chest with a knife during ritual sacrifices, and tearing out the heart. This was a rare practice in classic Maya days, resorted to only in times of dire stress, when it was felt that the usual offerings of crops and jewels, flowers, incense, tools, household implements and animals were not enough to appease the angry gods. At such times, even the classic Maya resorted to human sacrifice, and the "offering" was sometimes a willing victim who made this supreme sacrifice for the presumed good of the community. Later, under the Toltec influence, human sacrifice became more frequent among the Maya, and the victims were no longer volunteers but slaves and prisoners.

The priest-executioners who celebrated these bloody rites were called *nacoms*, the same designation that was used for military leaders in the civilian hierarchy. Like their secular colleagues, clerical *nacoms* were elected. Their election, however, was for life, probably because it would have been too difficult to get a new group of men every three years to take the grim job.

The *nacoms* were assisted by *chacs*, respected old men who attended sacrifices and other, more pleasant rituals, as the guardians of the community. *Chacs* participated, for instance, in the initiation ceremonies of girls and boys. On such occasions, a *chac* sat at each corner of the square that was roped off for the ceremony, to make certain that there would be no interruptions during the ritual. The most sacred duty of the *chacs* was to send the new year on its way by kindling a fire. The people loved and venerated the *chacs*.

Next to last on the ecclesiastical ladder stood the workaday priest who took care of the many tasks involved in the ritual-studded cycle of the Maya year. He was known as the *ah-kin,* which means "he, of the sun." While not regarded with intense awe or affection, the *ah-kin* was respected.

Below the *ah-kin* in social standing, but much closer to the people and better loved, was the *ah-men,* "he who understands." To call the *ah-men* a "medicine man," as some anthropologists have done, would describe his role but give it the wrong connotation. He was healer, counselor, and soothsayer in domestic matters. When appealed to in a just and moral cause, he could practice black magic as well, and inflict injury through bewitchment on persons who purportedly deserved such treatment. In the more remote highland villages of Guatemala, the *ah-men* exists and functions as he once did.

Nowadays, he has an extra task as well. He serves as mediator between Maya men and women and the saints in the village church who speak a different tongue and need to have the prayers of the people translated for them. Anthropologists describe the *ah-men* in this capacity as a "prayer-maker," but to the Maya, consciously or unconsciously carrying on a thousand-year-old tradition, the "prayer-maker" is a link in the long chain of *ah-men,* one who understands.

Except for the language problem, it is easy for the Maya to relate to the saints of Catholicism. The Maya have always believed that spiritual beings of one kind or another share their lives. In the classic days, they had their own theory of evolution. They thought of these spiritual beings as neighbors in the universe, a step up from man in the ladder of creation. Man himself was an advance from the animals, who, in turn, were up a notch of their own over plant life, which had its superior relationship with minerals.

The Maya believed in a single creator god who had made and
ordered the universe in this fashion, but they felt that this creator was
too remote and busy to pay heed to the daily existence of man on
earth.

Special gods minded human beings and their needs, their lives and
deaths, the Maya believed. The most senior of these divinities special-
izing in the affairs of mankind was Itzamna, a father figure comparable to the Greeks' Zeus and the Romans' Jupiter. Itzamna was the
lord of day and night and, as lord of day, was also the god of the
sun. By further extension, he was the god of wisdom and learning
and, in that capacity, the deity of priests and astronomers. Since wisdom and knowledge were passed down through the generations in
books, he was the god of writing as well.

Itzamna was venerated. The two gods the Maya loved best, however, were the god of rain, Chac, whose vital, life-sustaining function
is obvious, and the corn god Yum Kax, who is always represented as
a handsome young man, with an ear of corn either in his hand, or
sprouting from his ear or his splendid headdress. Yum Kax was
equivalent to the Greeks' Apollo, Dionysius and Demeter combined
into one adored deity. Finally, in the way of important deities, there
was Ex Chua, the dual god of warriors and merchants and, by extension, of all who traveled.

One of the two major goddesses was Ixchel, Itzamna's spouse, who
sent floods when she was angry but who was also the goddess of preg-
nancy and, Maya women believed, had invented the art of weaving.
The other goddess was Ixtab, special protectress of suicides, who saw
to it that persons who had taken their own lives went to their proper
place in heaven. Sacrificial victims shared that heavenly corner, as
did women who had died in childbirth.

The two most popular gods of the Maya
were the rain god Chac, shown here in
a version from Chichen Itza already
influenced by the Toltecs . . .

And the corn god Yum Kax, who
was always represented as a
handsome young man. This stone
figure is from Copan.

The gods, the Maya believed, resided in thirteen layers of heaven and nine segments of hell. Heaven included a paradisal segment for humans, where denizens sat under the shade of the sacred wild cotton tree, the ceiba, with food and drink always in easy reach, particularly sweet, thick cacao, fermented with a bit of honey.

Little was known about hell except that those who dwelled there were cold, hungry and miserable forever. Humans who had earned themselves such a fate went to the fifth layer of the underworld, where the presiding deity was Ah-Puch, the god of death. Ah-Puch appears frequently in the three Mayan books that have come down to us. He is a voracious looking creature, with a skull for head, ribs and backbone exposed in a spiny skeleton effect, and an expression that differs little from the Mephistopheles of medieval Europe. He seems to be sporting a possessive leer, and is clearly not a creature anyone would want to encounter in the dark.

The Maya believed, as did the Egyptians and Greeks before them, and the Inca after them, that the dead set off on a journey and should be furnished with supplies they might need for their travels: clothes and accessories; food; vessels to store the food, bowls and jars from which to consume it; and the tools of their trade. A tomb found in Tikal, beneath a temple, shows what an important traveler in the world of the Maya took on his celestial journey. The tomb disgorged plaques of jade and tubular necklace beads, bracelets, anklets and earplugs. It had a cache of baroque pearls, and a collar of jade made of 114 beads moulded into spheres that range in size from a half inch to several inches in diameter. The collar alone weighs eight and a half pounds and, with all the other jewelry added, this particular Mayan started on his trip to heaven with at least twelve pounds of adornment on his person. He was also equipped with twenty pottery

Another Maya god, clearly fat and prosperous, perhaps Ex Chua, dual deity of warriors and merchants. This clay whistle is said to be from Campeche, Mexico.
MUSEUM OF PRIMITIVE ART, NEW YORK

vessels, multi-colored and covered with designs. Among them were deep plates, a tall beaker, and a bowl, set on three feet, with fluting on two sides. The fluting seems to have been shaped to accommodate fingers. Possibly the bowl was intended for hot foods, with the fluted edges designed to be held between index finger and thumb. Vases had been added to the collection of vessels for esthetic purposes. One was made of alabaster, the other of jade mosaic. There was also an array of plaques, some encrusted with pyrite, to serve as mirrors. There were shells and stingray spines, and a number of incised bones, carved and colored with red cinnabar, which depicted some exquisite scenes.

One of these bone etchings displays what may well have been an artist's conception of the journey the buried man was about to take. It shows a long canoe, paddled by two divinities, one at the stern, the other at the bow. The craft holds four animals and one man. The animal travelers are an iguana, a spider monkey, a parrot

A canoe, paddled by two divinities, taking an important man across the river of death. An incised bone, from Tikal. UNIVERSITY MUSEUM, UNIVERSITY OF PENNSYLVANIA

with a human body, and a savage, furry animal that seems to come from as far down the evolutionary ladder as the parrot-man is up on it. Exactly at midships sits the man, clearly a personage of importance as indicated by his jade jewelry and his tall headdress, as well as his elongated profile and his thoughtful, self-contained expression. One of his hands rests lightly on the canoe's rim, the other gestures forward, as if he were reaching out toward that other world to which the two paddlers are carrying him. The boatmen apparently are the Mayan counterparts of Charon who, in Greek mythology, ferried the dead across the river Styx to Hades.

Life on earth, the Maya believed, had been created four times.

At first, there was nothing. Only the gods "moved among the four lights; among the four layers of the stars. The world was not lighted. There was no day. There was no night. There was no moon. Then they perceived that the dawn was coming; then dawn came."

Dawn was the first creation on earth, the Maya held, and produced the *uinal*, the length of the day. Perhaps this is why the Maya were so preoccupied with time and its reckoning. They saw in the *uinal* the beginning and essence of reality.

This is how the Book of Chilam Balam of Chumayel describes the first creation, in the rhythmic imagery characteristic of Mayan literary tradition:

The *uinal* was created, there at the dawn of the world. Sky, earth, trees and rocks were set in order; all things were created by our Lord, God the Father. Thus he was there in his divinity, in the clouds, alone and by his own effort, when he created the entire world, when he moved in the heavens in his divinity. Thus he ruled in his great power. Every day is set in order according to the count, beginning in the east, as it is arranged.

According to Maya myth, creating the planet had been easy, but man gave the gods trouble.

At first, the gods made men of mud. These mud beings could speak, but they were not very intelligent or strong, and they dissolved in water. The gods decided they could do better. The second time, they made men of wood. This was not satisfactory either. The wooden men were dry and bloodless, their intelligence was limited, and they lacked the inspiration to be appreciative of the gods who had created them. In fact, they behaved like blockheads, and the gods, disgusted, swept them away in a flood. A third attempt did not work out either. The creatures were ugly and cruel and their own implements—sticks and stones, pots, pans and grinding blocks—rose in revolt against them. Some samples of that third series survived. Their descendants, the Maya believed, are the monkeys.

The final, successful creation of man resulted when the gods used corn as their raw material, a mixture of white and yellow maize taken from a special place beneath a tall mountain and mixed into a gruel that could be shaped, and then be allowed to harden. The myth reflects the identification of the Maya with the corn that was their staff of life.

The Maya also had a close and meaningful relationship with animals. As in medieval Europe, where the unicorn symbolized purity and the lion prowess, so the Maya saw in the jaguar the essence of power, in the serpent fertility, and in the turtle, with its amphibious existence in the water and on land, an animal counterpart to man's own dual nature of body and spirit. Many Maya today still feel a special kinship with a particular animal and believe that they share a soul with it.

In Tikal, graffiti scratched into the walls and roofbeams of palace rooms show the intimacy of these relationships between animal and man. No one knows just who drew these graffiti, or why. Whether it was done for entertainment, or to propitiate the gods; whether they were meant to be decorative, or to have a magic effect. Dr. Michael D. Coe, one of the members of a University of Pennsylvania archeological team that has been exploring Tikal, speculates that:

From a religious point of view, these multitudinous graffiti could have had special and individual significance in the promulgation of magic. There exists the possibility of curative magic for illness, or troubles; of increase magic to make more animals and birds when they became scarce; or even to encourage the growth of crops after a crop failure of some kind. Family crests and totem animals of family lineages may have been presented to the deities, the artist seeking special favors or expressing gratitude.

Whatever the motive, the doodles demonstrate how close the Maya felt to the animals they knew. One of the palace walls has a jaguar, four-legged, spotted, with a very long tail, large round eyes, and a ferocious look. There is a deer, bright and whimsical, with its insides neatly sketched, down to the curl of a stomach. Close by, a

Temples and part of the ballcourt at Chichen Itza as they are today. Temple of the jaguars at Chichen Itza today.

BOTH, AMERICAN MUSEUM OF NATURAL HISTORY, NEW YORK

serpent slithers on the wall, striped, with a diamond-shaped head, its body twisted in curves and open-sided squares, its long tongue flicking. It looks very much like the snakes one can still encounter with unpleasant frequency in the rainforest. Another building has a more stylized doodle of a serpent, looking regal and wise and managing somehow to give the impression of a universal mother.

Religious ritual suffused Mayan life. Not only did it accompany every important act and occasion in human existence, it also filled the days of worship set aside for each of the important gods, and the periods of special obeisance which the Maya paid to each month of the sacred calendar. The Maya conceived of these months as divine burdens, carried by gods through eternity. Each god had his own timeload to carry for the duration of one month, after which he handed over his burden to another deity in a kind of relay cycle which, at fixed intervals, repeated itself. Mayan ideograms depict this concept. They show a god, looking very human on this occasion, carrying a timeload on his back like a large rock, sustained by a tumpline across the forehead. This way of carrying heavy burdens is still used in Maya lands. Nowadays, the burdens tend to be loads of wood or pottery, or even such items as a sewing machine or a phonograph. In ancient Mayan days, the load carried by the gods was a glyph of time, and each god was thanked and propitiated when he took over his burden.

Celebration started at dawn, when worshipers thronged into the temple grounds in the heart of the city to make their offerings, and to watch priests make the offerings of the community, on the first platform of the temple pyramid. In the stone chamber cresting the pyramid, the *chilan* meditated. After all offerings had been made, the priest emerged from his aerie to pass on to the congregation huddled in the plaza below the messages the gods had conveyed to him during his meditations. At the beginning of each round of the sacred calendar, the priest foretold what the year would bring in blessings and catastrophes, joys and suffering.

When the priests had concluded their part of the ceremonies, the dancers took over, in the plaza at the base of the temple. All dancing among the Maya was ritualistic. Some ceremonial dances called for as many as 800 performers at a time. Special dances existed for sowing, for planting, and for the harvest. There was a dance for the hunt, performed before the men set out, and again after they brought home their quarry. Big, important dances ushered in the new year and all other community celebrations. Sometimes individuals performed a private dance to plead with a deity for special favors, or to pay homage on a special occasion. One such dance, performed by a woman alone, under the new moon, was dedicated to love. It was known as the flower dance.

For important ceremonial occasions, dancers—men only—were fancifully costumed in flowing headdress and face masks; feather capes that produced a wing-like effect as the dancers moved; bells at their wrists and ankles; and in their hands either rattles and small drums, or flags and streamers made of colored cloth, painted parchment, or feathers. They stepped and swayed, pranced and whirled, thus saying grace, with energy and harmony, to the gods that provided the sustenance of the seasons and the rhythm of the planets.

Another integral part of a day of celebration was the sacred ballgame *pok-to-pok* which to the Maya symbolized the struggle between good and evil. The game is described in the *Popol Vuh* with the divine princes pitted against the lords of hell.

Pok-to-pok was played in a long, narrow court shaped like a

A pottery whistle in the form of a ballplayer
in helmet and belt. (From Guatemala)
UNIVERSITY MUSEUM, UNIVERSITY OF PENNSYLVANIA

capital I. The court was paved and two walls ran along the sides, with markers in the middle. The markers were carved rings of stone, somewhat like the ring that holds the net in basketball, but vertical. In *pok-to-pok* there was no net, and the point of the game was to drive a rubber ball through the opening in the stone rings. Two teams competed. The game required high skill because the players could not use hands or feet to maneuver the ball. They played with their torsos and their hips, around which they wore thick rubber belts. Since the ball was hard, fast and dangerous, they also protected themselves with masks over their faces. They looked a little like football players do today, except that their helmets tended to be plumed to display their status; their faces and bodies were tattooed to show their high social ranks; and the stakes of the game were quite extraordinary.

Pok-to-pok—the name probably derives from the sound the ball made as it hit the court's floor and walls—was observed by richly robed and heavily jewelled nobles from grandstands along the side walls of the court, and from small sanctuaries on top of the walls, usually built right above the goal markers, by priests. Since the winning team represented the triumph of good over evil, members of that team were entitled to the earthly goods of the spectators for whose benefit they had fought the good fight. Specifically, they had a claim on the portion of the earthly goods that the spectators had brought to the game. A Mayan noble dressed for a ceremonial occasion was quite a prize since his attire was likely to include a breechclout of jaguar pelt, a mantle of feathers, a plumed headdress, a necklace of jade, coral and pearls, anklets and bracelets of jade and shell, earrings, a belt buckle and possibly a breastplate carved of jade. All of these belonged by rule to the victors in the *pok-to-pok* game, provided the victors were sufficiently fleet-footed to snatch them off the departing spectators. One imagines that departure to have been quite a scramble, not in keeping with the slow dignity with which Mayan nobles usually carried themselves.

With the tensions and turmoil of the ceremonies at the temple, in the plaza, and at the game behind them, the Maya needed the rest of the day to relax and recover. They did this at banquets, for which a rich and varied table was set, honeyfire flowed freely, musicians played, actors performed, and conversation ranged to issues near and far, in space and in time. The celebration ended at dawn, when that first creation, the *uinal*, had run its complete course.

VII: ORDERLY, HARMONIOUS, EXACT

MANY MYSTERIES STILL SURROUND THE MAYA AND THEIR WAY OF life, but on one point there is unanimous agreement. Their arts and sciences were of a stature that entitles them to a permanent place among the highest cultures of mankind.

In the view of one "Mayanist"—there are persons who have devoted life-times of study to the Maya and their civilization—Mayan art is distinguished by three characteristics. It is, says J. Eric S. Thompson, orderly, harmonious, exact.

It is reasonable that this should be so. The Maya believed the universe to be orderly, harmonious and exact. Since their philosophy called for an understanding of the laws of the universe, and man's adjustment to these laws, it was logical for their art to try and capture an image of this order and harmony, an image on which they could feast both senses and spirit.

106

A good place to experience even today the impact of Mayan order, harmony and exactitude is among the ruins of Uxmal. Uxmal was a relatively late creation in Maya history, founded during the period of the New Empire, somewhere around 1000 A.D. Like many other Mayan centers, it is a kind of historic layercake. It seems that for a period in Maya civilization, temples were assigned life-spans, much like humans. A temple's life-span was calculated to encompass a mathematical ratio between two of the Mayans' calendars and it came out to exactly fifty-two years.

At Uxmal, one can see temples built one on top of the other, probably every fifty-two years, with the roof of one becoming the foundation for the next. Each ritual flight of stairs was filled in and plastered over to allow for another, larger flight of stairs to be built on top of it, and serve as a higher ladder to the gods of the sky. The result is a Chinese box of temples, one nestled in the other, each illustrating a half-century change in Mayan art.

The Maya built with concrete, which they made by mixing lime, lumps of limestone and a substance they called *sascab*, a marl composed largely of calcium carbonate. To the artistic and sophisticated eye of the classic Mayan, bald concrete had an unaesthetic appearance. The buildings therefore were faced with a veneer of well-cut stone. In Uxmal, a building known as the Palace of the Governors has such a stone veneer composed of almost every basic geometric form, fitted together into a mosaic façade. There are squares and diamonds, oblongs and triangles, plus the curves of a serpent's tail abstracted into a pattern resembling quite closely a Greek key. These mathematical forms are, in turn, surrounded by a border of leaves, the entire composition made of polished pieces of stone that look like marble.

Typical Maya friezes, decorating buildings above their doorways. This, at Uxmal.
MEXICAN NATIONAL TOURIST COUNCIL

The inside of a Maya temple, at Palenque, with a decorated crypt.
INSTITUTO NACIONAL DE
ANTROPOLGIA E HISTORIA, MEXICO

The frieze of the nobility in the "nunnery" at Uxmal.
MEXICAN NATIONAL TOURIST COUNCIL

It was the use of concrete that made possible the construction of the corbelled arch, one of the three features that distinguish Mayan architecture. Eight groups of buildings have survived at Uxmal, and each has at least one of these arched doorways. It is not a true arch, but a corbelled vault with two walls increasingly inclined toward each other. The effect is more like that of a Gothic church window—tall, narrow, soaring—than of an entrance or a gate. To build these arches, the Maya must have known the mechanical principle of stability, the tensile strength of concrete, and the theories of stress and strain.

The other two features unique to Mayan architecture are the roof-comb, splendidly displayed in the temples of Tikal, and the capstone that tops the corbelled arch and is frequently carved with a frieze, a figure, or a set of glyphs. One speculation holds that these capstones constituted an identification of the house, like a street number. The glyph on the capstone may have presented the name of the family that lived in the house or, if a figure was carved on the stone that topped the corbelled arch, it may have symbolized the deity whose name the owner of the house had adopted.

The most pleasing of the buildings at Uxmal is the group the Spanish conquerers dubbed "the nunnery" because it reminded them of a convent in structure and atmosphere. The complex of structures was probably a school built for the children of the Mayan nobles. The "nunnery" consists of four buildings framing a central court, all of them low, simple and elegant in line but with measurements just different enough to point up the individuality of each edifice without disturbing the harmony of the whole. The structure is like a melody of four tones.

The buildings are decorated with varying motifs, and these are instructive as well as pleasing. One edifice has a sculptured frieze of stylized *nas*, the simple houses of the Mayan peasant then and now. In Uxmal, the *na* is reduced to its basic lines, which are projected in white limestone and so constructed that they create their own pattern of light and shade. Another building—it constitutes the east side of the quadrangle—was dedicated to the nobility. It is decorated with garlands and crosses. To the Maya, the cross was a symbol of duality in balance. Nobility in human beings, the Maya held, evolved from maintaining a balance between the elements of man's given dual nature, passion and spirit.

Facing the edifice of the nobility is a building dedicated to the raw material out of which nobility is forged: mankind. The façade consists of an enormous serpent with a wide, open mouth. Out of this mouth pour people, to populate the earth, while the serpent's magnificent, curved body-tail stretches in sinuous circles across the remainder of the wall.

The building to the north, facing the edifice dedicated to the *na*, is consecrated to the rain god Chac, with his curled tongue, round and lush like the large raindrops that haunt men's dreams in the tropics. At one time all these friezes were painted in radiant reds, blues, yellows and greens. Chacs were always painted red because red was the color of blood and therefore of life, and no life was possible without rain. Now, only the delicate colors of the original stone remain: soft creams, buffs and terra cottas, marbled grays and a rose color like the needles of the henequin plant in the light of early morning. But the grass in the courtyard is still a luscious green and the butterflies that play around the buildings have wings of vivid yellow and red. They recall the days when the edifices matched the butterflies' hues.

The Maya loved form and color. They carved and painted not only their temples, palaces and schools, but their stairways, stelae and altars as well.

The best place to see Mayan sculpture today is probably Copan, in Honduras, where many carved stelae, a magnificent staircase, and some famous altars demonstrate the skill and sophistication of this aspect of Mayan art.

The stelae and altars of Copan also give us a visual insight into other facets of Mayan life. One of these carved ten-foot-tall stone tablets shows a personage, splendidly attired but of thoughtful mien. The sides of the monument are covered with panels depicting men at work. Some are carrying burdens with the aid of a tumpline across their foreheads. One is bent over, hammering. Another is asleep, fatigue etching his face.

A second stele shows a woman, in the full regalia of a *halach uinic*, with the customary jaguar breechclout converted into a skirt. She wears the usual masses of jewelry in her ears, around the neck, on the chest, about the waist, at the ankles and wrists, but they all have beads of bone in addition to the coral, shells and jade. From this we deduce that, at least during the classic period, it was possible for a woman to become both ruler and priest.

The most famous of the altars of Copan, Altar Q, gives an insight of a different type. The altar depicts sixteen Mayan scientists attending a convention. They are dressed in the costumes of their cities and they carry papers either rolled up or spread open in their hands. They are shown speaking or listening, arguing or thinking. The expressions on their faces look startlingly similar to those of modern scientists at a meeting. Some are arrogant, some smug; some thoughtful, some questioning. The men of Altar Q were astronomers, it

The reviewing stand, from which priests and nobility watched ballgames, was often flanked by sculptures. This kneeling figure, carrying what looks like an Olympic torch, is such a sculpture, in Copan.

A beautiful stele, with figures and glyphs, from Quirigua, Guatemala.

Another stele at Quirigua, threatening to topple. All Maya stelae were straight.

A set of ideograms,
carved in stone.

seems, who came to Copan from sixteen different city-states, sometime in the seventh or eighth century, to exchange information and
argue opinions. The altar commemorating their congress is placed
midway between two stelae, twenty kilometers apart, on opposite
hillsides. It is a calendric composition. The sun rises over the stele
on the eastern hill, stands straight above Altar Q at noon, and sets
over the stele in the west, on April 20. This is the time to prepare the
fields for the sowing of corn.

The sheer complexity of Mayan sculpture can be seen in Copan's
great stairway, also known as "the hieroglyphic stairway." It is a
flight of steps leading to a small temple structure, steps and balustrades decorated with 2,500 ideograms carved in stone. Since we
have not yet deciphered Mayan writing we do not know what these
glyphs say, nor why they have been carved on this particular flight
of steps. But we can admire the artistry of the Mayan sculptors who
shaped these intricate designs, without metal tools, more than a thousand years ago.

Painting among the classic Maya was even more ubiquitous than sculpture. It covered bowls and vases, plates, cups and jugs for domestic as well as ceremonial use, and the inside walls of houses and temples in addition to their façades.

One marvelous set of murals was discovered in 1946 inside a small temple in Yucatan. The sanctuary is called Bonampak, which means "painted wall" in the Mayan language. The building consists of three rooms, with the walls of each room, up to and including the ceiling, covered with frescoes that tell a continuous story. The paintings are not only vivid in color but graphically realistic in their portrayal of men, women, and children—their expressions, their costumes, and their actions. The frescoes show dancers impersonating earthgods, with a *halach uinic* and his family attentively watching the performance; a village raid and the capture of prisoners; arraignment of the prisoners before the *halach uinic*; and a sacrificial ceremony and dance.

Writer-explorer Victor von Hagen speculates on how the murals were painted, and describes their effect:

The technique is classic fresco. Cement was applied to the walls, and while it was still wet, the artist drew his outlines on it. Then his assistants—and there must have been many—applied the colors. Plasterers and artist have to work together in this medium . . . in a continuous process. The whole of the three rooms must have been painted in forty-eight hours . . . The figures are almost life size and give a sense of arrested movement as if they had been caught by a photograph.

The colors used by the Maya were both subtle and brilliant. They included the famous "Maya blue," really more an intense turquoise. It was made of a mineral called beidelite. Reds and pinks were derived from hematite, a crystalline iron oxide. A darkish yellow, in the

Maya carvings. All these were done in jadeite.
UNIVERSITY MUSEUM, UNIVERSITY OF PENNSYLVANIA

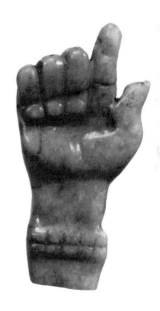

*Maya painting was exquisite, and the
range of colors wide. These are three painted
jars, all with a rim of ideograms at the
top and figures below.*

MUSEUM OF PRIMITIVE ART, NEW YORK (LEFT)
MUSEUM OF PRIMITIVE ART, NEW YORK (RIGHT)
UNIVERSITY MUSEUM,
UNIVERSITY OF PENNSYLVANIA (BOTTOM)

ochre family of colors, was made of hydrous iron oxide. Green was obtained by mixing yellow and blue. The Maya also produced a fine purple from mollusks, snail-like creatures that were used for the same purpose by the Phoenicians, whose employment of the dye in textiles gave rise to the royal purple. Finally, the Maya used a lustrous black, made of carbon; browns created by mixing black with various shades of yellow; a brilliant orange; and a range of terra cottas which they made by adding black to reds and yellows.

A self-portrait of a Mayan painter, or perhaps a drawing of a fellow-artist, was found in Poptun, a city in the Guatemalan rain-forest. It shows a man with his legs in the lotus position, the left hand holding an intricately shaped jar which apparently contained paint, while the right hand is poised for work, a brush between thumb and index finger. The hands have a delicate, feathery quality. The quality is repeated in bolder terms in the painter's headdress, which is so large and elaborate that it almost touches the ground. Since the size of a headdress was indicative of social standing in Maya civilization, the portrait reveals that painters were held in high esteem. The artist's jewelry—large earplugs and necklaces of sizable jade beads—confirms this impression. The face is a classic profile complete with almond-shaped eyes, prominent drooping nose, and sloping fore-head. The expression is one of total concentration.

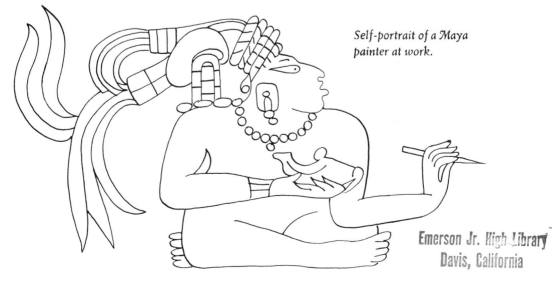

Self-portrait of a Maya painter at work.

VIII: THREE BOOKS SURVIVE

WRITING, LIKE PAINTING, WAS CONSIDERED A SACRED OCCUPATION and the Maya treasured their books. The artistry of the three original volumes that have survived is evidence of the devotion that went into their making.

Mayan books were brush-written, with black glyphs and ideograms, and illustrated in color. They were painted on glossy white paper, sized with a mixture of lime and the starch of a tuber. Writing brushes were made of tapir bristles, feathers, or human hair. The book was folded like a fan, with each leaf of the fan constituting a page. Chapters were written horizontally across the pages, covering as many leaves as were required by the chapter's content. A horizontal red line indicated a chapter's end. Like English, Mayan books

118

were written from left to right, and both sides of the page were used. The covers were made of wood, carved with glyphs and designs.

Human language generally progresses in three major stages. At first it is pictorial, with a rough sketch of a hut, for instance, consisting of a rectangle, topped by a triangle, standing for the word "house" or any other form of human shelter. Next, it progresses to the ideogram, when each drawn symbol represents an idea, and the glyphs become more complex and abstract. At that stage, the symbol standing for *tun*, the Maya calendar year, in conjunction with the glyph for water, which represents movement, would mean "once upon a time there was," and among the Maya was used to introduce a statement, a tale, a reckoning. The third stage is the phonetic one, when at first syllables and then letters represent the sounds of human speech, and make communication infinitely simpler and subtler. Mayan writing had evolved to the second stage and was poised at the third. It already contained some syllables.

From our still very fragmentary knowledge of the written language of the Maya, we can deduce that one of the three books that survived the Spanish conquest deals with astronomy. It is known as the Dresden Codex and its workmanship is exquisite. It was given this peculiar appellation because it somehow made its way to the state library of Dresden, Germany. The Russians found it there after World War II and took it to Moscow for study by Soviet Mayanists.

How it got to Dresden in the first place is another one of those puzzles that seem to surround our nascent knowledge of the Maya. We know that it was a present to the Royal Library of Dresden from the Emperor of Austria. It had been found in Vienna in 1739, perhaps after some Spanish soldier-priest had sent it home in the early years of conquest and occupation. The sixteenth century, when the

A section of the Dresden Codex.

conquistadors first came to the Americas, was the era of the Holy Roman Empire, when Spain and Austria were ruled by the same sovereign, who regarded Vienna as well as Madrid as his capital. Many documents and some treasure from the early days of the Spanish conquest of Mexico were found in Vienna. So, fortunately, was the Mayan book that has since become known as the Dresden Codex.

Two other volumes written by the Maya have been preserved. They are the Codex Paris, also known as Codex Peresianus, and the Madrid Codex. The Codex Paris was found at the National Library of Paris, in 1860, in a basket of old papers in a chimney corner. It is at the Paris Library now, in a more fitting place. The second appellation, Codex Peresianus, springs from the fact that when the book was found in that corner basket, it was wrapped in a piece of paper that had the word "Perez" written on it. Speculation assumed that Perez was the name of a Spanish soldier, or priest, who originally sent the book from America to Europe.

The Paris-Perez Codex apparently concerns itself with rituals and prophecies, such as the ceremonies and divinations that were part of the celebration of Pop, the first month in the sacred calendar year. Spanish writers of the sixteenth century report that they found books that record Mayan history. None of the three surviving volumes do that, as far as we can tell. Unless, of course, the prophecies can be regarded as history, since the Maya believed that time future was a repetition of time past.

The third surviving book, the Madrid Codex, is also known as Codex Tro-Cortesianus because the Spaniard who rediscovered the book in the sixties of the last century, believed that Cortez, the conqueror of Mexico, had personally brought the manuscript back with him to Spain. It is now in the Museum of Archeology and History in Madrid and it, too, seems to be concerned mainly with ceremonies and prophecies.

We owe the sad paucity of Mayan books to the Spaniards' medieval obsession with superstition and devilry, which in their minds covered all faith and ritual that was not Catholic. It seems that the Maya had libraries in each of their cities. They cherished these libraries, but the Spaniards considered them depositories of alien and dangerous knowledge, and burned them. We know this from the Spaniards' own accounts, particularly the records of Bishop de Landa who, in 1562, ordered that all Mayan books in his diocese be obliterated. In classic inquisitional style, he destroyed them by fire, and made a symbolic occasion of the event. He sent soldiers to collect all the books they could find and bring them to the town of Mani, in Yucatan. There, he had the books built into a pyre and set to the torch, surrounding the conflagration for religious emphasis by "many Indians . . . suspended by their arms, and some of them by their feet, with stones hanging from their feet . . . And friars whipped them and spattered them with tapers of burning wax."

The description of the event comes from Bishop Landa himself, who concludes his account with a brief summary of what the volumes contained, and with the astonished notation that the Maya did not seem to enjoy his book-burning ceremonies.

Landa, referring to the Maya of Yucatan, says:

These people also made use of certain characters or letters, which they wrote in their books of ancient affairs and their sciences, and with these and drawings and with certain signs in these drawings they understood their affairs and made others understand them and taught them. We found a great number of books in these characters, and as they contained nothing in which there was not to be seen superstition and lies of the devil, we burned them all which they regretted to an amazing degree and caused them affliction.

As most of the arts, music too had religious significance for the Maya. Music was a form of worship, an integral part of every sacred ceremony. Mayan music would sound repetitive to our ears, but it was rich in instrumentation and tone. Rhythm was carried by drums, of which there were four kinds. The most sonorous was a stand-up kettledrum made of wood that was usually carved, with a stretch of jaguar or deer hide across the top. It was tall, reaching to the chest of the player, who beat it with his fists. Its sound was deep and carried far. Another version of the kettledrum was low and large,

A stand-up kettledrum.

so large that the player could sit on it cross-legged and, again, beat it with his fists. There was also a horizontal drum, with two hide-covered surfaces which were struck by wooden beaters tipped with rubber to produce a lighter, faster tempo. Finally, the Maya employed two kinds of small hand drums. One kind, also made of wood and hide, was used by dancers to accompany their steps, along with tinkling anklets of copper bells; the other was a beautiful instrument made of the shell of a small land tortoise, lacquered and carved. Its sound was evoked by striking the shell with the palm of the hand.

Melody was carried by trumpets and flutes. The trumpets were enormous, often taller than the men who played them. They were constructed of wood or clay and had smaller, natural cousins made of conch shells. Flutes were shaped of clay or bone and came in many forms, including ocarinas with godheads, and simple, five-tone Pan-pipes of bone.

To lend variety to their orchestras, the Maya also had an array of rattles fashioned from bones or gourds, and a series of raspy instruments of ceramic or wood, cut to produce sounds similar to those that can be evoked from a washboard or a comb. Music and song usually accompanied each other, the singers carrying the melody along with the flutes and trumpets, while hummers provided rhythm in unison with the drums.

Drama was a separate and quite different art. It was as secular as any art could be in the lives of such a deeply devout people. It concerned itself mainly with historic or heroic encounters, much as Greek drama did and, like Greek drama, it was performed with masks. The actors and audience suspended disbelief to respond to the role indicated by the mask, however fantastic. Also like the Greeks, the Maya had a sharp sense of humor in their theatre, and were quite capable of producing pungent political satire.

A Maya actor. His helmet mask is at his feet. (From Jaina Island, Mexico)
MUSEUM OF PRIMITIVE ART, NEW YORK

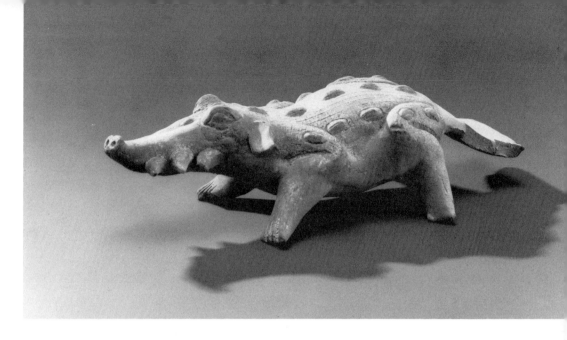

Playful Maya art: an alligator made of clay, from Mexico.

After the conquest, when the Spaniards felt sufficiently secure to take the risk, they sometimes asked Mayan actors to put on a play satirizing the conquistadors. The Maya complied, and the tradition continues to this day. The sharpest, most incisive comment on the foibles and follies of Guatemalan politics does not come from the pens of commentators, cartoonists or even playwrights, but from the Indian communities who put on their own drama on festival days, with the audience chuckling at every well-aimed barb.

The Maya genius also found expression in the lesser arts, in the fashioning of weapons, tools and household objects, both useful and decorative. The Maya fashioned their tools from flint and their weapons from obsidian, which is a volcanic glass the color, most appropriately, of dried blood. The flints were gray or green, and were used as knives, spatulas and blades; obsidian went into arrow-heads and spear tips. Both materials were sometimes chiseled into intricate shapes to serve as offerings, the flint often leaf-shaped, the obsidian flaked into jagged-edged designs with a striking resemblance to some modern sculpture.

Obsidian blades, all from Tikal.
UNIVERSITY MUSEUM
UNIVERSITY OF PENNSYLVANIA

Ideograms, incised on bone.
UNIVERSITY MUSEUM,
UNIVERSITY OF PENNSYLVANIA

Ideograms, carved in stone.

We still cannot decipher the Mayas' written language.
But the ideograms below are a sample, perhaps telling the
story of the figure shown in the middle.

Carved wooden lintel, used in Maya palaces.
This one comes from Piedras Negras.
UNIVERSITY MUSEUM,
UNIVERSITY OF PENNSYLVANIA

A Maya seal, probably representing a quetzal.

For their houses, the Maya collected incised bones, and designed mosaics of shell and coral, pyrite and jade, mother-of-pearl and rock crystal. These seem to have served the same decorative purposes in their homes as paintings or pieces of sculpture in our living rooms.

The Maya also designed stamps and seals. The seals were incised either with a glyph that may have been the name of a family or a city, or with recognizable patterns of such realistic objects as a corn cob or a quetzal. Stamps were used on paper, on cloth, on leather, and even on the skin.

From sculpture and paintings we know that the Maya had baskets woven of rush, in many colors and complex designs. The baskets were used in the home and for marketing. Heaped with food, they were also deposited in tombs to nourish the dead on their journey.

Feathers had many uses among the Maya. In addition to making up headdresses, mantles, and capes, they were also woven into tassels for breechclouts, and bracelets for the upper arm. Balls were made of feathers, looking much like shuttlecocks in a badminton game. And there were feather fans, crests, panaches, and canopies indicating rank and status by the length and brilliance of the plumage. In the jungle or the highlands, the Maya were surrounded by birds, and they liked imitating the birds' colors, song and spirit.

A Maya stamp.

IX: THE PLANETS IN THEIR COURSE

MAYAN SCIENCE SEEMS TO HAVE SPRUNG FROM AN INTELLECTUAL orientation more concerned with the abstract than the practical, more fascinated by theory than by its application.

The Maya, for example, had conceived of the wheel. They had even constructed wheels. But because they thought of the wheel as a symbol of the sun, of the roundness and reassuring dependability of that star, they considered it blasphemy to put the wheel to use for such mundane purposes as the hauling of goods or the carrying of persons. It is equally characteristic of the Mayan imagination that it saw nothing wrong with putting wheels into children's toys.

The Maya also made use of the wheel, in an appropriately abstract and highly sophisticated way, for their calendrics.

The Maya had three calendars. One was the sacred year, which centered on their image of the days and months as burdens carried by gods, with each time segment partaking of the characteristics of the deity that bore it. Human lives were influenced by these characteristics, the Maya believed, and days or months were therefore good, bad, or indifferent, fortunate and unfortunate. Mayan ritual was geared to the sacred calendar, designed to please or placate the gods and thereby influence the impact of their burden on man. The sacred calendar had thirteen months of twenty days each.

The second calendar calculated the natural year, defining the exact passage of time required for the earth to make its annual revolution around the sun. This process varies by fractions with the location on earth from which the movement is measured. In the tropics, near the equator which is our planet's widest diameter, the year is exactly 365.2422 days. We have determined this by using the most sensitive scientific instruments. The Maya, through their observations, had reckoned the year at 365.2420 days. They made this calculation without instruments of any kind, using only their eyes and their minds.

To make this natural calendar fit into their own neat patterns of arithmetical order, the Maya divided it into eighteen months of twenty days each, plus five days, with the fraction adjusted with a leap year mechanism every fifty-two years.

The third Mayan calendar was a purely mathematical one. It involved calculations of time that swept back past all of man's history into the pre-history of the planet to the mysteries of the universe itself.

This third calendar was fixed at an even 360 days, which made it easy to manipulate the kind of time that truly concerned Mayan scientists, periods that reach back as far as 400,000,000 years. A glyph on a stele in Quirigua, Guatemala, depicts such a calculation.

The three calendars—sacred, natural and mathematical—were thought of as wheels, with spokes that interlocked predictably at fixed intervals. The sacred and natural calendar coincided every fifty-two years, and the Maya considered fifty-two years a normal life span. They described it as "a year bundle."

The double wheel of sacred and natural calendar in turn coincided with the mathematical calendar in what archeologists now call the Mayan long count. The three wheels of the long count interlocked every 260 years. The Maya called this time span a *katun*. The glyph for *katun* was made up of two figures, both quite elaborate, one faintly reminiscent of a Mayan ball player encased in his mask, the other looking somewhat like a jaguar head in profile. The Maya thought of each *katun* as a completed cycle in human affairs, with history likely to repeat itself after each cycle.

Katuns were numbered in a series of one to thirteen, and each *katun* was believed to have a specific character. *Katun* number eight, for example, was a period of political change and it was the knowledge that *katun* eight was upon them that made the Maya Itza give up and surrender to the Spaniards and Christianity in 1697.

What, exactly, did the Maya count with the aid of their three calendars?

Glyphs signifying the Maya katun, *a span of time which lasted 260 years.*

The sacred calendar was a reckoning of individual man's fate. Each day in it had a name and was associated closely with a deity. The name itself was personified, and carried the male prefix *ah*. Even now, a Mayan who still lives his traditions refers to days in this manner. It is as if he were to say: "Mr. Monday is coming up. He is a lucky day. I will therefore start a new venture."

The names of our own days have a not dissimilar origin. They derive from planets which were thought to influence man's fate. Monday is a contraction of moon day. At one time, the moon was held to be a major influence on man. Similarly, Saturday is a contraction of Saturn day, and Sunday obviously was named after the sun.

The Maya also had names for each of their twenty-day months, and each month carried its burden of fate. Each day had a glyph of its own, the design intimating the message. The glyph of a very lucky day, for example, is a pattern of intertwined circles and curves, creating an impression of smooth, round harmonies. The glyph of an unlucky day, on the other hand, is broken up, with three fragments scattered about, one displaying pointed teeth like an upended comb, the other exhibiting sharp corners and a nasty-looking protrusion in the middle, while the third part just sort of sits there, inchoate and isolated. The three segments of the glyph look like pieces of the proverbial Humpty Dumpty before anyone thought of putting him together again.

Glyphs for a lucky day (left) and an unlucky one (right).

Birthday celebrations, as well as all other major ceremonial occasions such as initiation ceremonies or marriages, were determined by the sacred calendar. The deity that governed the day of a person's birth was held to exercise a major influence throughout life, and was an important determinant in the choice of occupation.

The natural year governed the agricultural season—sowing,

Glyphs of the days in the twenty-day month.

Imix   *Ik*   *Akbal*   *Kan*   *Chicchan*   *Cimi*   *Manik*

Lamat   *Muluc*   *Oc*   *Chuen*   *Eb*   *Ben*   *Ix*

Men   *Cib*   *Caban*   *Eznab*   *Cauac*   *Ahau*   *Ahau*

planting and harvesting—and also the time for hunting and fishing.

The mathematical year was concerned with history. For convenience, the Maya picked a day far enough back in the past, from which they reckoned the development of man. It was set at 3113 B.C.

Other civilizations have based their time count on similar suppositions. Jews count history from a point very close to that of the

Names and glyphs of the months. Pop started the year and the first day of Pop was celebrated.

Pop   Uo   Zip   Zotz   Tzec   Xul

Yaxkin   Mol   Chen   Yax   Zac   Ceh   Mac

Kankin   Muan   Pax   Kayab   Cumhu   Uayeb

Maya, 3761 B.C., which is posited as the year in which the creation was accomplished. The Greek Church, also trying to fix a time of creation, comes up with 5509 B.C. The classic Greeks, preferring in such matters calculations of known events to hypothetical assumptions of unknown occurrences, counted time in Olympiads, four-year periods which culminated in the celebration of festivals. The Greeks were able to trace such festivals back to 776 B.C. They were even able to cite the names of the victors in each Olympiad. It is as if we were to decide to reckon our days by the World Series, as far back as we can remember the name of the pitcher responsible for winning the pennant, agreeing that time was really not worth counting before that. The time count we use is, of course, also a historical convention, based on the presumed birthday of Jesus.

The Maya claimed no historical event for their starting date, in either human or planetary terms. At least, not as far as we know.

They were, however, painstaking in their observations and calculations. The basic assumption was, once again, that the universe was orderly and harmonious, that planets therefore moved in definable patterns, and that these patterns could be understood if observed with sufficient devotion and accuracy. Mayan observatories during the classic period were a structural expression of these assumptions. A court was laid out, consisting of a pyramid and three temples. The pyramid was built on the west side of the court, facing due east. It supported a building, which was usually round, with a veranda encircling it. Directly opposite the pyramid, the three temples were lined up on a platform in a straight north to south line. They were so positioned that, from the observation point on the pyramid, the sun rose directly behind the center of the middle temple on March 21, which is the vernal equinox. On June 21, the summer

The round building is the Maya observatory at Chichen Itza.
Maya town planning was always harmonious, often symmetrical. The
buildings here, a restoration of Chichen Itza, are lined up in a
straight north to south line. Such an arrangement was used for astronomical
observation. Both are restoration drawings by Tatiana Proskouriakoff

PEABODY MUSEUM, HARVARD UNIVERSITY

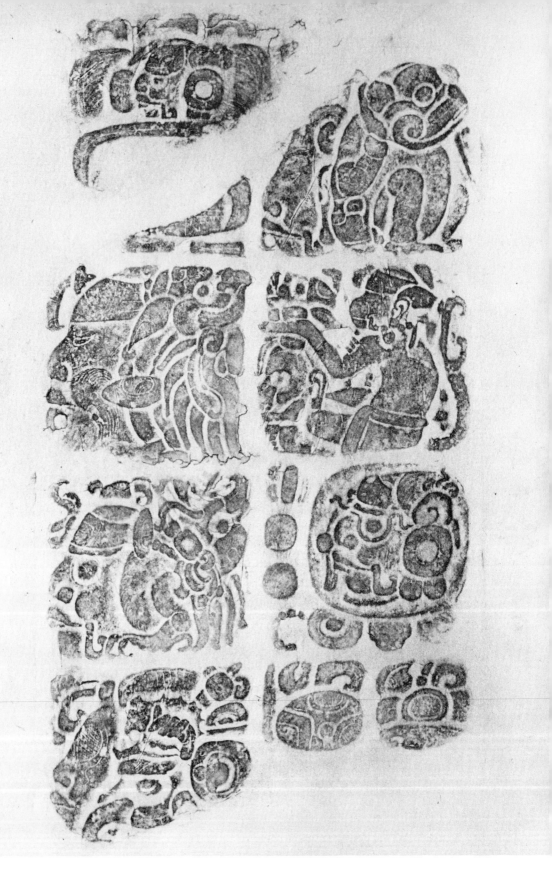

*Maya ideograms. These are rubbings from a stone
lintel in Chiapas. Do they deal with astronomy?*

solstice, the sun rose behind the north front corner of the temple on the left, and on December 21, the winter solstice, it came up behind the south front corner of the temple on the right. The astronomer located on the pyramid, keeping a daily watch of the sun's movement in relations to the three temples, could observe with complete accuracy the relationship of sun and earth.

Tracking the movements of Venus was more complicated, but the Maya managed it. They came up with a Venus round of 584 days. Modern astronomy puts it at 583.92 days.

It took teamwork to achieve such accuracy, with team members covering both time and distance. Observations were made and recorded over generations, and astronomers in various parts of the Mayan realm conferred regularly to tally their results. The famous Altar Q of Copan apparently represents a congress of astronomers debating and checking their findings.

The Maya also recorded their planetary observations in books. The Dresden Codex, to the extent to which we can decipher or interpret it, deals with astronomy, primarily calculations of the Venus cycle.

Mayan calendrics and astronomy required complex calculation as well as detailed observation. For this purpose, the Maya created a system of arithmetic to which, given its time and place, only superlatives can do justice.

Its greatest achievement was the invention of the concept of zero. We take it for granted now but the Greeks, the greatest mathematicians of Western civilization, never thought of it. Nor did the Romans. The Arabs, who were also acute at mathematics during their golden age, did not invent but at least borrowed the concept from India. The Maya both invented and used it. Their symbol for it

Maya mathematics were based on the vigesimal system, i.e., multiples of 20. A dot represented one, a bar five. Zero was a special figure, looking something like a football. The system, zero to 19, is illustrated at the right.

0	1	2	3	4
5	6	7	8	9
10	11	12	13	14
15	16	17	18	19

Numerals had their own glyphs, also ordered into a vigesimal system.

0 . 1 2 3 4 5

6 7 8 9 10 11 12

13 14 15 16 17 18 19

was a shell. It looks like our zero lying on its side, with some vertical lines through it.

Also unlike the Greeks and Romans, the Maya had numbers. (Contemporary civilizations used letters, and for an idea of how cumbersome a system that was all you have to do is look at the Roman rendering of a date.) A dot represented one; a bar, five. Nine, for example, would have been written as four dots topping a horizontal bar. The system was vigesimal, which means that it was based on multiples of twenty rather than the multiples of ten that we use. With dots, bars and zeros, figures could be written very simply, with multiplication sequences running 1, 20, 400, 8,000, 160,000, 3,200,000, 64,000,000, 1,280,000,000 and on. We know the Maya counted at least as far as the last of these because, in addition to numbers, they also had a glyph for each figure in the multiplication sequence.

In their own way and for their own purposes, the Maya were also good engineers. They built roads, bridges, reservoirs for water, and insulated storage bins for crops.

The Mayan road system is not as famous as that of the Inca, for whom roads were the lifelines of empire, much as they were for Rome. The Maya were interested in roads mainly for two purposes: They wanted to facilitate travel to religious centers, and they wanted to reach the coast so that they could journey from there by sea to visit fellow-Maya up and down the Central American isthmus and in the peninsula of Yucatan. They used roads, rivers, and the sea for trade as well, but trade was a secondary consideration. The primary purposes of the Mayan communications system were religious and scientific, to share in the communion of worship or exchange the data of science.

The roads give evidence of the purposes they served. They were high, wide and handsome. They consisted of causeways, built up from the ground to a height of two to five feet, and were constructed of rocks and boulders, weighing from twenty-five to three hundred pounds each. The rocks were imbedded in limestone, then covered with limestone gravel. The gravel was wetted and tamped down with rollers, which gave it a smooth, even surface. A Mayan road roller was found at Coba, a city in Yucatan, known for the network of roads that leads to its center. Coba has sixteen such roads, some still recognizable as highways. The Coba roller is a cylinder made of limestone, about thirteen feet long, with a diameter of close to two and a half feet. It weighs five tons and was clearly capable of crushing limestone gravel to provide a smooth topping for a highway.

Unlike Inca roads, which were built a uniform width of twenty-four feet, Mayan roads varied in dimension, possibly with the importance of the ceremonial center to which they led. Some causeways measured only a narrow fifteen feet across, while others were twice as wide. The widest Mayan highway discovered to date is thirty-two feet, and extends a little over sixty-two miles.

Like the Inca, the Maya maintained road houses along their highways, to feed and rest travelers and store goods. The Maya also built altars along the way, where travelers stopped to pray, and to make small offerings to Ek Chua, the god of merchants and of all who journeyed.

The major, and very characteristic, difference between the roads of the Inca and the causeways of the Maya is that in the Inca empire all roads belonged to the ruler, and everyone traveled them at his bidding, and his mercy. Mayan highways were dedicated to the gods. They were extra-territorial in the sense that they did not belong to the cities to which they led, and could provide sanctuary for anyone who needed it. If a Mayan required asylum, he was safe the moment he reached a causeway.

Another interesting difference between Incan and Mayan roads is that the Inca planned their highway system much as we design thruways today—to get from one population center to the next in the quickest possible way. The Maya planned their roads with a more esthetic purpose in mind. Mayan causeways meander, like country lanes, and seem designed to offer vistas whenever possible: views of trees and lakes and, when they approach a city, glimpses of pyramids and platforms, temples and palaces.

Even the conquistadors were struck by the beauty of the Mayas' highways. Spaniards chronicling their journeys on Incan roads, focused their description on how these fantastic highways climbed over towering Andean peaks and stretched across plummeting ravines. In Maya country, the conquistadors wrote home about "handsome causeways" and "roads bordered with fruit trees."

In addition to building handsome highways, the Maya had also developed a construction system that produced roads and bridges with amazing speed. We have the Spaniards' word for both. Sometime after the conquest, in 1564, the Spaniards wanted to run a road in the Yucatan Peninsula from Merida to Mani. It is a distance of fifty miles, and the Spaniards decided to turn the job over to the Indians. The road was completed in three months, with no more than 300 men working on it.

Forty years earlier, when Hernando Cortez, the conquerer of Mexico, had occasion to travel through Maya country, he needed to ford the Usumacinta River with his men, their horses and their baggage. The Usumacinta is a sizable stream, and Cortez wanted to cross it near what was then a large Maya city, Iztapan. He asked the ruler of Iztapan to have his people build a bridge. The ruler agreed, and the bridge was completed in four days. Not an easy man to impress, Cortez wrote home on that occasion: "It [the bridge] contained more than a thousand logs, the smallest of which was the thickness of a man's body. . . . Horses and men passed over it . . . I do not know what plan these Indians used to build this bridge; all that one can say is that it is the most extraordinary thing one has ever seen."

Some Mayan causeways have survived in good condition. Chichen Itzá has such a road. It leads to the notorious *cenote* which doubled as water reservoir and sacrificial lake. The causeway was built when the Maya had already succumbed to Mexican influence and is, by Mayan standards, a rough, uncouth kind of a road.

More typical of the classic Maya are the causeways of Tikal, wide and smooth, their limestone topping glowing silvery-white in the rainforest. In Tikal, some causeways double as walls of a large reservoir, itself lined with limestone. The reservoir as well as the causeways are intact.

When the Maya traveled by water, they did so in canoes, usually fashioned from the trunk of a single tree. The trees of the rainforest reach giant size and the Maya worked these mammoth trunks into sea-going craft, holding as many as forty persons: rowers, traders, passengers. Christopher Columbus encountered a Mayan sea-going canoe, examined it closely and described it as being "as long as a galley, eight feet in breadth, rowed by twenty-five Indian paddlers."

The Maya traveled the length of the Central American coast on both the Caribbean and the Pacific sides. On the east coast, there is evidence of their journeys carrying them as far north as Tampico in

Mexico and south to the islands off Venezuela, a distance of close to 3,000 miles. Mayan canoes were customarily made of cedar, and a number of cities seem to have specialized in shipbuilding. The vessels were curved upward in bow and stern, and outfitted with a rudimentary, triangular sail. Fundamentally, however, they were row boats, moved by oars on long sticks with leaf-shaped tips. The Maya tended to hug the coast in their sea travels, wending their way along chains of ports they had established on both sides of the isthmus. The ports served as trading stations.

To prevent their running into coastal shoals or rocks, the Maya set up buoys of floating banners, topped by feathers, that glittered their cautionary messages under the sun. At night, the Maya traveled by following the north star.

The most basic of the Mayas' scientific accomplishments was their agriculture. Debate still rages over whether we owe corn, the staple of all pre-Columbian civilizations, to the early peasants of the Andes or to the Maya of the Guatemalan highlands. There is little doubt left, however, that the Maya were the first to cultivate the cacao bean with all its delectable uses, as well as the papaya and the avocado.

The Maya also knew how to tap trees for rubber, of which they manufactured soles for their sandals, and balls, belts, and faceguards for their games of *pok-to-pok*. Apparently they used rubber also for poultices, along with copal wax and tar.

Chewing gum, too, seems to have been a Mayan invention, with resin obtained from the same chicle tree we use today. Mayan boys rolled the resin into balls to chew, or covered the balls with lime, let them harden in the sun, and used them to play marbles.

X: MAYAB,
THE NOT MANY

SINCE MOST OF THE MAYAN GLYPHS HAVE NOT YET BEEN DE-
ciphered, great areas of knowledge are still missing about this fascinating civilization. One of the gaps is the word Maya itself. We are
not certain what it means, or why the Maya chose to call themselves
that. A Mexican author-anthropologist, Antonio Mediz Bolio, who
has written an excellent book about the surviving Maya and their
way of life in today's Mexico, says the entymology of Maya consists
of *ma*, meaning no, and *yab*, meaning many. Maya, he holds, is a
shortening of *mayab* and means the not many, i.e. the special, the
chosen.

It is an interesting hypothesis, and Mayan attitudes and achievements would certainly justify the appellation. Mediz Bolio has a
poetic perception. He believes the Maya are a special people still.

148

Writing of them today, he says: "The ear of the Indian listens to what the wise birds say, when the sun is setting. He hears the trees speaking in the silence of the night; he hears the stones, gilded by the light of morning."

About five million identifiable descendants of the Maya are alive today—one third the number that constituted the Maya realm during the Golden Age. Roughly half of these Maya are in Guatemala, where they make up nearly two-thirds of the country's total population. Sizable communities also exist in Honduras and British Honduras. There are a few Maya descendants in northern El Salvador, and close to one million live in the southernmost Mexican states of Yucatan, Quintana Roo, Campeche and Tabasco. The Maya in Mexico are the survivors of the New Empire. In Guatemala and Honduras they are the direct descendants of the people who, during the classic period, were responsible for the scientific and sculptural marvels that can still be seen in Copan and the architectural glory and ritual magnificence that survives in the ruins of Tikal.

Most Maya have been converted to Christianity and are now officially Catholics. However, they perceive Christianity in such purely devotional terms that they can fuse their ancient beliefs with the concepts of Catholicism and infuse many of their traditional rituals into their Christian worship. One group of Maya, the Lancandon, were never converted. They still hold most of the classic Mayan beliefs—to the extent to which they have been able to preserve these through oral tradition—and their religious, social and personal relations continue substantially unaltered from the ancient ways.

How long Mayan ways will endure under the world-wide impact of television and the transistor radio is uncertain. But today, anyone visiting parts of southern Mexico, mainly in the Yucatan Peninsula

*Maya faces today. Above, a man and woman of the
Lancandon group, who were never converted to Christianity.
Below, a Maya woman sitting by a fallen stele.*

where Maya communities have kept to themselves, can see not only remnants of Mayan glory, but the living continuation of Mayan ways. Some Yucatec faces, long, lean, finely cut, with aquiline noses and almond eyes, look as if they had stepped down from the murals of Bonampak or a stele in Copan. The clothes women wear in these Yucatan communities are the one-piece chemises of the ancient days, with openings for the head and arms, embroidered at the neck and sometimes at the hem. In Guatemala, where each Maya community has its own particular costume, the cut of the clothes shows the Spanish influence, but the varied and subtle color combinations in the fabrics are clearly Mayan and the designs woven into the long skirts and knee breeches, the shirts, blouses and jackets, the stoles and waistbands are traditional and have come down from classic times.

In Yucatan and Guatemala, the baked-mud-and-thatch huts, clean swept and utterly simple, with their backyards in which a few animals are raised and spice bushes grown, look exactly like the dwellings depicted in drawings of the tenth century that were found at Chichen Itza, or the stylized *na* houses carved into the frieze of the "nunnery" in Uxmal. Even the classic steambath still exists in many Maya communities and helps to account for the meticulous cleanliness of these people in their isolated villages that are often still without tap water or sewage pipes.

In such Maya villages in Guatemala, farmers still spend the night before the sowing of the corn in a vigil of prayer, song and meditation. At dawn, they set out together, with their sacks of golden seed kernels, which they drop methodically and reverently into the *milpa*, the maize field that, they still believe, originally yielded the substance of which man was made. They do this with a planting stick that differs in no way from the tool their ancestors used.

Maya women and children in the
backyard of their homes in the
Guatemalan village of San Antonio
Aguas Calientes. The name of the village
is Spanish but the people and their
customs are Maya.
UNITED NATIONS

A Maya man, wearing modern clothes
but worshipping in the traditional
way, in a cave on a mountain top in
Guatemala. NATIONAL TOURIST BUREAU,
GUATEMALA

Maya in Chichicastenango, Guatemala, still pay homage to deities in the old ways, with white and red petals strewn on the ground, along with fragrant pine needles, and *pom* incense, made of tree resin, swirling in clouds of attention-demanding pungency. In Chichicastenango, this worship now takes place in church, with the saints of Catholicism looking down on the old ceremonies. Crops are brought to the altar to be blessed, with a Mayan "prayer-maker," an *ah-men*, fulfilling his traditional function.

The direct, intimate relationship that connected Mayan man with his gods also survives. The Maya believed that the gods, when they come to earth, prefer dwelling places that are high and secluded, so that their favorite residences are caves on mountain tops. There are such caves in the Guatemalan highlands, and on certain nights, determined by the sacred calendar, descendants of the Maya still climb the mountains and spend the hours of darkness in a grotto communing with the ancient gods.

Finally, a visitor today can still walk into a Guatemalan village, where a Maya community has preserved its way of life, and the harmony is palpable. It almost leaves a taste on the tongue, and certainly a subtle and lasting impression on the spirit.

We are told that in man's reach from the known to the unknown, if he uses his mind, we get science, if he uses his heart, art results from the quest. The magnificence of the Maya is that they used their hearts and their minds, and thereby achieved a high art as well as an advanced science.

In their small corner of the planet, in a time span that was short as human history is reckoned, the Maya, took their own giant leap in the exploration of space: external, objective space, as well as the internal, subjective space that makes the mystery of man.

PART II

XI: ITZAMNA

ITZAMNA WOKE TO THE HOT SPRING MORNING HUNGRY AND EX-
cited. It was new year's day in Tikal, the first day of Pop, when the
gods delivered their messages to the priests on what the future of
the coming four seasons would hold. Itzamna's uncle was a priest.
For seven days, he had sat in a small stone room at the top of his
temple, eating only corn mush and taking a few sips of water, to concentrate on hearing the heavenly messages. The priest sat on a reed
mat with his legs tucked under, "folded within himself," he had told
Itzamna. Pop was the word for mat, he had pointed out, and because
a great deal of man was water, there was a natural affinity between
man's understanding and the mat made of reeds. That was why the
first month of the year was called Pop. It was the month of understanding.

156

Itzamna's uncle had drawn the glyph of Pop on a piece of parchment with the delicate hairs of his brush dipped in a carmin-colored dye. It had looked intricate, the plaited of the reed mat on one side, a cross in a circle on the other, the whole encased in what resembled a human head resting securely on two legs. The cross represented the duality of life, the priest had noted, because in life everything had two aspects: light and dark, good and evil, beginning and end. The circle, however, was the universal perfection that encompassed all contradictions and superseded all opposites.

"Complicated," Itzamna thought. There were times he wished that he had not been born on the particular day of the particular month in the particular year that made the astrologer decide that his name should be Itzamna, and his profession that of a scribe. Itzamna was the god of night and day, an ugly old man with down-curling lips and a long drooping nose, of whom everyone expected understanding. The expectation tended to spill over to anyone named Itzamna. Young as he was, people had a habit of discussing with Itzamna their problems and confusions. And Itzamna's uncle assumed without question that the boy would comprehend the difficult symbols and meanings that absorbed his own priestly life.

Itzamna had often felt that he would have preferred to be named after the corn god, who was young and handsome, and whom everyone adored. He had, as a matter of fact, been told that he looked like the corn god, and from the portraits he had seen on books and on stelae, it was true. The corn god and he had the same broad, clear forehead, the same almond-cut eyes and acquiline nose, long straight hair falling down the back, broad shoulders and slim torso. They also had the same large, flat ears with long lobes that lent themselves so well to wearing big earplugs of jade which reminded everyone of the green shoots of corn in the spring.

The thought of corn made Itzamna's stomach growl. The week preceding Pop was a week of fasting and abstention. For Itzamna, it meant that he could not soak in the family's steambath at the back of the garden and was allowed only a quick catwash with cold water before every meal. And meals were sparse. No deer or turkey, no doves or wild currasow; no meat of any kind. Just corn and vegetables and fruit. These were available in great variety: squashes and pumpkins, sweet potatoes, avocado, many types of beans, and of course corn in many forms, from gruel and toasted patties to lumps of maize hardened with lime that could be chewed when one got hungry between meals. Fruit, too, was ample: melons and mulberries, papaya and sapote. But Itzamna missed his favorite drink of chocolate and corn, with a little red pepper sprinkled on the top. To Itzamna, nothing really tasted good without chili, made from the dark red pods his mother's kitchen servant grew in the garden behind the house. The pods were grated into a powder in a special dish with a fish incised at the bottom which served as grater. Itzamna particularly liked that dish, with its bowl painted sacred blue, soft like the water in a shallow pool on a warm summer day. He also liked the fiery taste the red powder gave to the bland squashes and beans, and the tingling feeling it left on his tongue. To mix that fire with the bittersweet thickness of a chocolate drink, or drown it in the freshness of a beaker of mulberry juice, was Itzamna's idea of a meal. He had had to forego them the past week. No spice was permitted during the fasting period.

It was difficult not to think about such matters, although Itzamna knew he was not supposed to. The purpose of the fasting period was to purge oneself of everything extraneous and distracting, and prepare body and mind for the rituals of new year's day: the sacrifices, the message the priests would bring from the deities, the dances, the ballgame.

Excitement washed over Itzamna as he thought of the events to come. He rose to dress. Deciding what to wear was not easy. He would put on his embroidered breechclout of course, the one with the feather design in the front and tassels in the back; the tooled sandals with the high ankle guards; and his feather cape, made of the plumes of toucans, pheasants and wild turkeys that he had snared himself. It had taken the better part of a year to trap the birds in the thickets of the forest. Still, he had been lucky. The birds he caught had produced very handsome feathers, bright red and shimmering green, a blue more intense than the sacred blue, and a yellow as golden as the sun at midday. His mother had carefully arranged the plumes on a backing of soft cotton and they made a brilliant cape. There had not been enough feathers for a full length mantle, but he was too young to wear one of those anyhow. A cape reaching just below the waist was proper at his age.

Itzamna hung the cape on his shoulders and twirled full circle. The garment fluttered like a bird on the wing.

The bird-like sensation sent his thoughts in a new direction. The feathers with the most delicate colors were those of the hummingbird. He had been tempted to catch at least one, to use its plumes for the fastening of the cape. He had refrained because he knew a girl who was named after the hummingbird, and ever since he had first seen the girl he had not been able to aim a pellet at her namesake. Kukul was the girl's name, and Itzamna thought it echoed the sound the hummingbird made in its tiny throat as it hopped among the leaves.

Kukul, it seemed to Itzamna, really was like the bird in many ways. She was small, round, lovely, and quick to flit in and out of sight. Her people were hunters and farmers, and lived away from the city's center. Still, Itzamna managed to catch a glimpse of Kukul now and then, when she came to the market with her mother. When Itzamna went hunting, the part of the forest where Kukul lived always seemed the most likely place to catch what he wanted. And on the rare occasions when Itzamna walked far into the forest, to the round stone tower where his grandfather, the astronomer, worked and spent most of his life, Itzamna almost had to pass Kukul's family compound. The causeway was very close to it. It was nice to step down from the hard surface of the paved highway and walk for a stretch among the lichens and leaves on the soft ground.

Kukul just might be at the market today, Itzamna speculated. Festival days were always an attraction for shoppers. Merchants came in from all over the realm on holidays to bring their wares to Tikal. On festival days, the market stalls offered much more than the usual corn, cotton, cacao and salt. The traders brought stingrays and shells from the coast, which women liked as ornaments and for their sewing. From the highlands, they carried obsidian, black and violet and mulberry blue, to be used in knives and spears. They offered gold from the far south, shaped into little animals, stars or nuggets. Sometimes on holidays, the important merchants even displayed quetzal feathers, two feet long and more brilliant than any pheasant's or toucan's. But only the priests and the nobles could wear those. Still, Itzamna thought, they were beautiful even to look at, and perhaps he and Kukul would be looking at them together today.

Considering this possibility, Itzamna decided to make quite certain that his appearance was perfect. This required jewelry. You could tell a man's social standing by the precious stones he wore. Itzamna considered his earrings of shell and coral. They were nice, but not significant enough for this kind of a day. New year was a day for jade, the sacred stone. Itzamna did not own any jade earplugs as yet, nor a jade buckle. His parents thought he was still too young for such important ornaments. But he did have a jade pendant, small— the size of his thumbnail—but of a beautiful deep green and exquisitely incised with the features of the corn god, the deity everyone thought he resembled. The pendant was a present from his uncle the priest, who had given it to Itzamna following a particularly difficult writing lesson. Itzamna treasured the jewel. That would have been a good reason to wear it on this important day, but Itzamna planned to attend a ballgame and when the game was over the members of the winning team had the right to help themselves to the spectators' clothes and jewels. And those ballplayers were fast, muscular men.

But the jewel was appropriate for the occasion Itzamna thought, holding it against the lobe of his ear, where it nestled, a rich green against copper brown, looking truly like a corn shoot in freshly dug earth. He held it up against his nostril. It looked even better there. More prominent, too, with the resemblance between him and the corn god clearly visible. But, Itzamna considered, clearly visible to the ballplayers as well. And a nose ornament was easy to dislodge. Too easy, Itzamna speculated regretfully.

He was about to put the jade back into its reed box when an idea struck him and made his eyes sparkle.

He had been told they looked like cacao beans, and when he was excited he tended to intensify his elegant squint and then they felt like his favorite drink of chocolate and chili, a sensation of sweet smarting. He could feel it now, as the idea came to him of a way in which he could safely wear his jade. The pendant had a small hole drilled into the top. Itzamna took the strong thong of his sandals for daily wear, ran the leather string through the hole, and tied it in a tight knot at the back of his neck. That way, the jade came half way down his chest, where it looked splendid. No one could miss it.

His problem solved, Itzamna completed his costume by putting into his nostril a small topaz his father had brought him from the last trading journey. Two disks of polished pyrite, a gift from his mother, he attached to the back of his head. His mother had several large pyrite disks, which she used as hand mirrors. His disks were tiny, but they did catch the light and, when the sun struck them, made specks of color dance over his blue-black hair.

He could hear his mother's voice at the back of the house, and the clatter of dishes. She was directing the servants to collect bowls, platters, plates and beakers that had been used during the year. These would be taken to the sacred meadow within the hour, and offered to the gods, after being ceremoniously cracked. For tonight's feast, every dish would be as fresh and new as the new year.

Well, Itzamna thought, almost every dish. There were some particularly beautiful pieces, like that chili grinding dish with the fish at the bottom, and a deep bowl the color of dawn that had a jaguar's head as the knob of its lid, which his mother would not break and send to the meadow. At least he hoped she would not. He never quite knew each new year's day just what he would, and would not, find when he returned home at dusk. When he was younger that had distressed him. Now, at fourteen, Itzamna knew that while old, familiar things were reassuring, new things, and new experiences, were exciting.

An important new experience was in store for him this day. He had been invited to attend his first ballgame. It was a special treat because it was a new year's game, when the best players were in the court, the stakes highest, and the *halach uinic* himself would be watching, along with the senior priests and the ambassadors who had arrived during the preceding week from other important cities. He would undoubtedly be the youngest as well as the least important person at the game, and he owed the invitation to his uncle, who had conducted complicated negotiations to obtain it.

When Itzamna stepped outside, everything smelled moist and fresh. The night's heavy dew had been soaked up by the morning sun but at this early hour remained as a sparkle in the air. The causeways, too, sparkled. They had been swept clean, and the white limestone glowed. The city's ordinary streets, of dark, trodden earth, had been covered with sweet-smelling boughs and blossoms.

Hurrying toward the temple, Itzamna soon caught the first pungent whiff of incense. He flared his nostrils and breathed deeply. Itzamna liked incense. It seemed to enter his being like a cloud, sharp and sweet at the same time, enveloping him inside. While it made his eyes smart, it also gave him a floating sensation, as if he were a cloud. His uncle had explained that indeed this was one purpose of incense, to make a man feel less himself and alone, and more like the particle of the universe that in truth he was. The other purpose of incense was to please the gods. The gods liked offerings from man. Itzamna had been taught that the Heart of Heaven had created man so that he could praise and worship the gods. In return, the creator gave man life and sustenance. On this first day of Pop, Itzamna's uncle would tell the people of Tikal what kind of life and sustenance they could expect for the coming year. That was why the priest had spent those

secluded days and nights in his stone cell on the top of the temple:
to prepare himself to receive the divine word, and pass it on.

Itzamna did not tarry as he walked by the market. A quick glance
around the square, into the stone stalls where the important merchants assembled their goods, and along the neatly arranged mats in
the open, where the lesser traders displayed their wares, had shown
him that Kukul was not there. He could not have spoken to her
if she had been. It was not proper for men and women to speak to
each other in public. They could have exchanged glances though.
His heart skipped at the thought. But Kukul was probably at home
now, helping her family prepare their offering for the sacrifices.

Itzamna had tucked his own offering into the waistband of his
breechclout. It was an arrangement of flowers, one flower for each
of the twenty months of the divine calendar. He had made strenu-
ous climbs to far treetops, and ventured deep into dark and dangerous
parts of the jungle, to get the blossoms he wanted. They constituted
a vivid arrangement of colors and scents, harmoniously composed.
None dominated the others by either smell or hue. They blended,
and in the blending enhanced each other. Itzamna had chosen the
flowers with careful thought as well as intense effort. He hoped the
gods would be pleased, and that the small pleasure he offered them
would merge with the gifts of all the other people at the sacrifices
to delight the deities. He hoped, too, that the gods would manifest
their delight by sending sun and rain in due measure, rather than
drought or floods, as they had in some other years he remembered.
Perhaps, Itzamna thought, his own deity would have time this year to
fulfill some of his special desires. The god Itzamna might help him,
for example, to write a complete page of a book. It was a difficult
task, but how pleased everyone would be if he managed it!

Itzamna felt that he might just be in a position to get some special attention from the gods in the year to come. They could not help but notice him today. He had received permission from his uncle to assist one of the *chacs*, the priests who performed the rituals of the day. He would swing a censer while the offerings were presented, first carefully placing the pungent *pom*, shaped like a heart and painted in the sacred blue, into the clay brazier. His father had given him three *pom* hearts for the purpose, as well as the censer. It was new, and a work of art. It looked like a mask, was painted in many colors, and had small holes cleverly worked into the design that emitted the incense. It was not easy to keep swinging the heavy censer for two or three hours. Itzamna knew that his arm would get very tired. But it was a great honor to be assigned this task and, Itzamna admitted to himself, it also afforded a marvelous vantage point from which to see the *halach uinic* and the splendid gifts he would bring.

When Itzamna reached the first temple platform where the offerings were to be received, activity was already intense. The word had come that the *halach uinic* was on his way from the palace. Itzamna barely had time to fill his censer, saying the appropriate prayers as he did so. He had just begun to swing it in his far corner of the platform, when the ruler's retinue appeared on the causeway. Itzamna found it difficult to get a full view of the *halach uinic*. The ruler sat in his palanquin, shadowed by an enormous fan of feathers, which a minor lord swayed gently to make certain the ruler was wafted by a cool breeze. The *halach uinic* was followed by ambassadors, each in his own, smaller palanquin, and their retinues. From afar, the procession looked like a glistening snake.

At the edge of the temple grounds, the *halach uinic* left his palanquin, and Itzamna could see him clearly. The tassels of the chieftain's jaguar breechclout swept the ground, as did his brilliant feather mantle. He wore a belt as broad as the span of Itzamna's hand, and its buckle of deep green jade was the size of Itzamna's face. It looked, Itzamna thought, like a green sun. On his chest, the *halach uinic* sported a necklace of jade beads, each bead the size of a dove's egg. The necklace had a medallion in the center that matched the belt-buckle in size and in its verdant glow. Anklets, bracelets and earplugs repeated the pattern.

If the jade made the ruler look like a green sun, what about the headdress? "It is the rainbow," Itzamna thought, "come from the sky to earth for this day."

The plumed crown towered high above the *halach uinic's* aristocratic face with its magnificent curved beak of a nose and expanse of sloping forehead, long ears, and deeply drooping lower lip. The brilliant feathers cascaded down the ruler's back, below the waist, in a glitter of multi-colored waves.

The *halach uinic* approached the steep, narrow stairs leading to the temple platform. He climbed them alone, on foot. On each step, he paused to pray. The ambassadors followed him at some distance. When the *halach uinic* reached the platform, he fell to his knees. Like every other citizen of Tikal, he approached the place of sacrifice with his eyes cast down, his offering extended in his hands. Itzamna could not make out precisely what the gift was. All he could see was a magnificent bowl, heaped with jewels. The ruler held the offering up to the sky for a moment. The sun struck it and Itzamna thought the gods had smiled. Then the *halach uinic* set his offering down on the place of sacrifice, where it was enveloped quickly in incense and smoke.

Just what happened during the subsequent two hours, Itzamna could not later recall in detail. An endless stream of people flowed up the narrow steps, silently addressed the gods, left their offering, and flowed down the stairs to the plaza below. There they stood, tightly packed, taut with terror and hope, waiting: waiting for the priest to bring them the heavenly message containing their fate for the year.

Itzamna felt the tension rise toward him. It mingled with the incense, gripped his solar plexus, and seemed to wind his stomach into a coil. He was overwhelmed suddenly by the feeling that the flowers which had seemed so fine a gift, really were not enough. More was required of him. He transferred the censer to his left hand—it seemed strangely weightless—and reached for a stingray that a poor fisherman had just left at the edge of the sacrifice grounds as his offering. Itzamna ran the sharp prong through his earlobe, first one, then the other. Blood quelled from both, fell on the ground in a few drops, then coagulated on his ears. He did not wipe it off.

"Like earrings," he thought, "earrings for the gods."

He felt light suddenly. As his uncle had told him he would, he felt as if he were a part of that cloud of incense that seemed to grow and reach out to embrace the world.

In that cloud, at its apex on the very top of the temple, a figure began to take shape. It drifted like a wisp of mist out of the cave-like darkness of the chambers that constituted the temple's crest. The outlines sharpened as the flowing form slowly descended the stairs to the platform of sacrifice. It was Itzamna's uncle, the priest, his face gaunt and sallow, his loose white robe smudged with pieces of dank earth and bits of ash that clung to him. He seemed to have difficulty walking, and his eyes, when he came close enough for Itzamna to see them, looked like the deep water cisterns in the heart of the jungle: endless and empty, except for a dark light that came from no one knew where. Close up, Itzamna recognized the features, but he did not feel that he knew the man. This was a being from another world, a messenger of the gods.

Down in the plaza, the people had become very still. Their breath seemed to come in unison, reaching Itzamna's ears like the sigh of a storm-laden wind. Heads were turned up, eyes fixed on the priest. No one moved. Into the strained silence, the words of the priest, slow and heavy, fell like the first drops of rain on the parched corn furrows after the dry season.

"The gods will send . . . ," he began.

As in most years, the divine message turned out to be a mixture of blessings and tribulations. There would be enough rain to harvest the crops, and no floods would swamp them. No tremors of the earth would occur, and the planets would move calmly in their course. But there would be man-made catastrophes. A war in the north was likely, with slave raids by the barbarians that would catch some Maya in their net. In the highlands, fellow-Maya, wresting their sustenance from the not-always generous mountainsides, would be very busy tending their crops and might not have time to spare to dig for jade and obsidian, and trap their usual quota of quetzal birds. And in the south, the primitive people, who erected no stelae and traded in gold, would be meaner this year, and demand more cacao beans and copper bells for their shiny baubles.

The priestly message had been delivered. As the last words rolled from the platform to the plaza, in what sounded more like an echo than a human voice, the crowd began to stir. Voices rose, some in sorrow, some in jubilation, some in concern, some in relief.

Itzamna, too, felt the knot at the pit of his stomach ease. He became aware of the strain in his muscles caused by the hours of swinging the censer, and felt a sharp pang of hunger. His throat was dry from the smoke. He would have liked to leap down into the plaza, as he had been told a puma leaped from a tree.

Had others the same desire? It seemed that way, because just as Itzamna was about to lay down his censer and descend the steps, dancers filed into the square below. There were nearly a hundred of them, their faces sheathed in masks of birds and animals, bells at their ankles, banners in their hands. Slowly, as the drums pounded, the flutes trilled, the trumpets blared and the caracols murmured, the dancers formed a pattern, fluid but repeating, in squares, circles and crenellations. They stepped carefully and gravely, because each movement was a prayer, each pattern dedicated to the gods who saw it, knew it, and wanted it precise, exactly as tradition prescribed. Itzamna knew the dancers had rehearsed for weeks and would perform for hours without stop, until nightfall when the gods would have had their fill of worship and the dancers, like everyone else in Tikal, would settle down to feasting till dawn.

As he watched the rhythmic configurations, Itzamna could feel the tension gradually leave his body. The dancers' deliberate movements, the circle of colored pennants, the weaving line of masks and bells undulating to the edge of the plaza fascinated and soothed him. He could have watched forever.

Until he remembered: The ballgame! It would start at high noon, and a quick look at the sun standing almost upright above him showed the time was near. Itzamna bowed slowly, ceremoniously, to the *chac* he had assisted, then scampered down the steps backside first, like a monkey.

At the ballcourt, most of the spectators had already assembled. As Itzamna had anticipated, they were the cream of Tikal society: nobles, important priests, the leading merchants, architects and artists, and important visitors from other cities. He could tell the strangers by their rich jewelry—visitors wore the very best they owned when they went to a ballgame in another town—and by the extra proud tilt of their heads. They maintained this posture to indicate that while they had come to Tikal to worship and pay homage to the *halach uinic* of this magnificent metropolis, they, too, represented Mayan cities of splendor and achievement. Itzamna knew that among them was the envoy of Copan, the city in Mayadom that was dearest to his grandfather, who said that the astronomers and mathematicians of Copan were the most knowledgeable in the land. Itzamna's grandfather had once traveled to Copan—a journey of many days and nights—to attend a congress of astronomers. He had returned replete with satisfaction over what he had learned and most respectful of his Copan colleagues.

Itzamna's eyes swept over the polished stone benches. He recognized many faces, but there was no one to whom he would have dared to speak. They were all dignified people of position and at least twice his age. Quietly, he slipped into a corner seat on the highest row.

The game was breathtaking. Both teams maneuvered the little black ball with such skill and speed that Itzamna found it hard to follow. It flew in arcs and curls along the court, bouncing from the glistening limestone floor and the polished and painted walls.

The players looked grimly intent. *Pok-to-pok* was a sacred game, Itzamna knew, representing the eternal battle between the forces of good and evil, the powers of heaven and hell. He had also been taught that, as in these profound and perennial struggles, all victory was only temporary. But very important.

The spectators were as intent as the players, their spirits as well as their eyes mesmerized by the game. Points piled up on both sides. Once the ball rose high and close to one of the stone rings and the spectators gasped. Putting the ball through one of these rings was the culmination of the game and brought immediate victory to the team that managed it. But the opening in the rings was small, hardly larger than the ball itself, and making the ball soar through it was like entering the gate of heaven—a rare achievement.

When it did happen that new year afternoon, no one was prepared for the event. It came as the highpoint of a team play which had involved three mounting curves of the ball, one sent off by a player's knee, the next by another's elbow, and the third, the miraculous one, by the captain of the team using the rubber belt around his waist. The ball reached for the ring in a wide, incredibly beautiful arc, seemed to pause for a second in front of the ring and, while the spectators froze in wonder, passed through the hole and dropped, quite slowly, to the ground.

A wild melee followed. Later, Itzamna remembered only that he heard a gasp—it must have come from his own throat—and tried to slide down the balustrade of the grandstand as if it were a tree. No one paid any attention to him until he reached the court and tried to run along the sidelines to the exit. The triumphant players had more important treasure to capture. For a few moments, Itzamna thought he might get away free. Just as he reached the end of the court, however, one of the players—young himself, Itzamna noted—spotted the jade amulet with the corn god on it. As Itzamna had intended, the amulet was attractive and noticeable.

Should he make a run for it? Itzamna wondered. If he did, the player would very likely catch him. Thoughts raced each other through Itzamna's mind. If the player decided to yank at the thong to get the pendant off, Itzamna might well get choked and certainly hurt. On the other hand, Itzamna did not want to face the player and let himself be stripped of everything. The player would certainly grab the topaz in Itzamna's nose, and the handsome cape. Itzamna made a quick decision. He ducked low to get out of the player's reach, pulling the pendant over his head at the same time. He dropped the pendant to the ground and, as he had hoped, the player stooped to pick it up, giving Itzamna his chance to escape. But he did not get away quite as he had planned. The player was close enough to catch hold of his flying cape. He pulled hard, the cape gave at the fastening and fluttered down beside the amulet. Itzamna did not turn around. He sprinted out of the court and did not stop running until he was on the crowded causeway that led to his house.

At home, Itzamna did not immediately go to his room. Instead, he went to the steambath at the back of the garden. He knew the bath would be empty at this hour and he could slip into it unobserved. His parents would have taken their bath much earlier and were by now entertaining new year guests in the living room. They would be sitting on low stools drinking *balche*, that fermented honey drink that loosened everybody's tongue and made Itzamna dizzy. They would be talking at this stage, mainly about the offerings they had made and what they hoped these would bring in response. Later, conversation would turn to the men's most recent journeys, the goods they had bought, the people they had encountered. Later still, when everyone had warmed to each other under the influence of the *balche*, they would speak of their adventures on these journeys, and in the far reaches of the land. Finally, when the *balche* had made them voluble and careless, they would speak of administrators and tax collectors and rulers, here and in other cities, and what was right and wrong with them all.

Itzamna liked that part of the men's talk, and today it would be more pointed and witty than usual because a group of actors had been hired for the evening—he had heard his father make the arrangements—and the actors' pantomime almost always dealt with unnamed rulers and their foibles. The trouble was that by the time the men got around to this kind of conversation, it was usually late in the evening and Itzamna could no longer keep awake. Especially if he had consumed some *balche* himself. Since he had undergone his initiation rites a few months earlier, he was permitted to take *balche* on ceremonial occasions. In truth, he still preferred his *chacau haa*, the cacao, corn and chili that stung the tongue. *Chacau haa*, however, was not served on feast days and even if it had been, Itzamna would probably not have voiced his preference.

At the moment, the consideration was a theoretical one. He could certainly not appear in company the way he looked, with his face and legs scratched and smudged, his breechclout covered with ashes, his knees bleeding from his precipitous drop to the floor of the ballcourt, and his throat red and smarting from the player's yank at his cape. He did still have the topaz in his nostril and the two drops of blood on his earlobes. He was glad of these now; perhaps they were truly the most precious jewels of all.

He took off his clothes in the outer room of the bath and entered the steam chamber. How soothing it was there. He stretched out on the bench to let the vapors envelop him. A steambath, he had been told by his parents, was not only a physical but a mental cleaning as well. It brought rest and peace. At this moment he needed both.

Lying on the smooth bench, troubling thoughts at first floated through Itzamna's mind. Perhaps it had been wrong of him to want to bear the corn god's name instead of his own. Perhaps the wish was vanity and the deities had reminded him today that they did not approve of vanity in man. That might have been the reason for his losing his two favorite possessions, the pendant and the cape. Being called Itzamna had its own rewards that one should treasure. His mother had often commented how appropriate the name was, because Itzamna also meant lizard and she claimed that he really moved like a lizard, quickly, in and out, so that you never knew just where he was. More seriously, she had pointed out to Itzamna that the lizard was of the same family as the crocodile which, as everyone knew, lived in the deep waters and carried the earth on its back. Right now, slithering on the warm bench, it seemed to Itzamna that being a lizard was perhaps not such a bad fate.

Later, when he joined the celebrations in the living room, the feasting was already in full sway. He had meant to rest for only a few moments after the bath, but had fallen asleep on his bed of woven hidestrips and dried grass. It was probably the smell of the hay that had sent him slumbering. Anything sweet-smelling made him think of Kukul, and the forest, and the last thought he had had before dropping off was that he would go to the forest that night to call on his grandfather, rather than stay at the party. He could pass Kukul's house on the way. Anyhow, trekking to the observatory in the jungle seemed like a fitting end to this portentous day, and a proper beginning for the new year.

When Itzamna finally appeared in the living room, he wore a fresh breechclout and his ordinary sandals. They were comfortable, and it would be a long trip to grandfather's. His cape gone, Itzamna took the coverlet on his bed and folded it into a mantle. It would give him protection in the forest, and that was all he needed tonight. The jungle was full of its own jewels in the dark: fireflies, bits of the moon and the stars flitting through the treetops, and the soft glow of airplants fixed like lamps to the low-sweeping lianas.

Sitting down to his parents' banquet, Itzamna was served quickly with a bowl of curassow stew, well spiced with chili, and a cup of *balche*. With his eyes, he asked the servant to give him mulberry juice instead. She smiled conspiratorially and brought it, a tall beaker full. No one else paid him any attention. The men had been eating and drinking for some time. They were talking now, with the quickened, slightly blurred speech he recognized as *balche* talk, their eyes bright, their gestures more expansive than usual. The actors had already come and gone, but the musicians were still playing in the room next door and occasionally one or two of the men would get up and dance. The musicians had also had their share of *balche*. Their music crashed like a waterfall, and sometimes it rose to a crescendo that made conversation impossible.

Itzamna set out for the jungle as soon as he had eaten. The causeway was silent. Everyone in Tikal was either still celebrating or already asleep. The year had been long and hard for many, the week of fasting demanding for all. Now that the gods had assured them of another year of life and sustenance, they could enjoy good fellowship, dance, sing, or rest. Itzamna wondered whether he was the only one on the causeways of Tikal that night.

As always, he left the highway to walk past the compound of

Kukul's family. There, the sounds of carousing were unmistakable. The men in Kukul's family had harder years than most people he knew, working the earth, trapping animals, making tools in the winter. In their lives, every day was crammed with demands and dangers, and the seasons were both friend and enemy. The priest had given them good news today: no drought, no floods. They had reason to celebrate.

Where would Kukul be at this hour? Itzamna wondered. In the kitchen, helping to cook and serve, or asleep after a long, busy day? He hoped she was asleep. She was really too young and small to be working as hard as she did. Itzamna meant to do something about that some day. It would not be easy, but he would find a way.

He was glad now of his own, unplanned rest in the early evening. He always forgot just how long a way it was to grandfather's. Back on the causeway, the road seemed to Itzamna particularly hard, high and lonely. Moving along on it did not make him feel in the least like a lizard. Just the opposite. He felt upright and isolated, and a little shivery. When the massive tower of the observatory finally came into view, he was very glad to see it.

He found his grandfather on the terrace, bent over a parchment covered with dots, dashes, and ideograms. Itzamna knew these to be calculations of the courses of the planets. Grandfather and other astronomers like him throughout Mayadom had observed the planets for generations, recording and figuring what they saw. They sent folded parchments to each other, and left books to their successors. It filled Itzamna with awe to think that his grandfather probably knew as much—and cared as much—about the movements of the stars in the sky as his mother did about the comings and goings of her servants, or his father about the trading of goods in the realm.

The parchments, his grandfather had explained to him, represented an account of time immemorial. Time itself did not really exist. It was merely a mathematical convenience, grandfather had said. Itzamna did not understand how this could be. His days were made up of time, and they began and ended. He did know, however, that his grandfather had reckonings of planetary movements that went back nine million years, and other scientists had calculated time back to four hundred million years. This was one reason why his grandfather suspected that time really had no beginning. And no end. Men just marked off portions of it for their own guidance. And perhaps the gods did the same.

Itzamna often could not follow his grandfather's concepts. Grandfather's world seemed so vast, and his ideas, while they were simple and clear when he explained them, had so little connection with the world as Itzamna knew it, by touch and smell, hearing and taste, that it was difficult to make sense of them. Still, Itzamna could see the stars with whom his grandfather seemed to converse as if they were his brothers, in a language of dots and dashes, and that strange glyph that looked like a seashell, which his grandfather called zero. And, it was good to sit beside grandfather on the wide terrace of the tower, and watch him look up and out, or bend silently over the parchment.

After a while, grandfather stopped his work and brought from the room inside the tower a drink of mulberry juice that he had warmed up, some toasted corn patties, and black bean paste, sprinkled with chili. It was simple fare, but it tasted marvelous to Itzamna. It warmed him in the tepid night and, strangely, made the faraway stars suddenly seem closer.

"What a fortunate boy you are," grandfather said as they were eating, "to be named after Itzamna, the god of all this." His long, bony hand swept across space, east to west. The arc it drew covered what they could see of the sky and the myriads of stars glittering in it.

Itzamna did not respond to his grandfather's comment. But shortly after they had eaten, when he had spread the sleeping mat on the veranda and had covered himself with the cotton mantle that had become a coverlet again, the canopy of stars was the last sight he saw before his eyelids fell, heavy with fatigue. The last sound he heard was his grandfather saying, "Good night, Itzamna." At that moment, the name seemed to him to contain the twinkle of the stars and the vastness of the sky.

XII: KUKUL

KUKUL'S DAY BEGAN LESS THAN THREE HOURS AFTER ITZAMNA'S
ended. When she entered the kitchen, barefoot and moving quietly so
as not to wake up anyone else in the family, it was still dark in the
house and outside. Kukul's house was oblong and rounded off at
both ends. The kitchen was on the left, separated from the living
and sleeping quarters by a wall of saplings and mud and constructed so that the warmth of the hearth could seep into the entire dwelling. The heat was welcome in the cool evenings of the rainy
season.

The hearth also wafted the smell of food through the house, and
the men of the family liked that, particularly when they came home
from a day in the fields or the forest. They were always ravenous

179

then, ready to eat twenty corn patties each. Satisfying those appetites required a lot of kneading, shaping and tossing of dough, which was done by Kukul and her mother.

Kukul's first task each morning was to light the three-stone hearth. It was set against the wall in the center of the kitchen, flanked on each side by shelves that held the family's eating and cooking utensils. These consisted of grey-brown bowls and plates that could be stacked into each other, a number of clay beakers, and the plaited reed fan that Kukul used to stir up the banked ashes of the fireplace.

Kukul felt her way along the rounded wall to the hearth. When she was a little girl, she had liked the kitchen. "It looks like a pumpkin sliced in half," she had once told her mother. Her mother had smiled and said that was a good way to think of it. Pumpkins were nourishing, and that was what a kitchen should be.

With the glints from the hearth to help her see, Kukul took from the larder—another set of shelves along the wall—dried strips of deer meat, pieces of smoked monkey, and some chunks of cured wild turkey. From a large clay jar, she fetched a mass of corn paste, which she shaped into balls and carefully sprinkled with chili. She wrapped the corn balls, along with the three different meats, into a thick palm leaf. That kept the food cool and protected until noon when the men unpacked it in the fields for their lunch. It was an elegant lunch and Kukul felt a little extravagant fixing it. Usually the men only had corn for lunch and perhaps one strip of meat. This day, Kukul decided, they deserved something better.

Like everyone else in Tikal, the men in Kukul's family had celebrated the new year, had drunk much, spoken loudly, sung and danced until late. But they had not started any quarrels and, more important yet, had not set fire to the house. Kukul still remembered how, two years earlier when she was ten, the priest had predicted all manner of travail for the year, and the men celebrating the first night of Pop had been disturbed and angry. Angry enough to get into a fight, and disturbed to the point where one of them, in a fit of fury had kicked over the hearth and deliberately blown the sparks into the roof. The thatch was very dry at that time of the year, and the roof had caught fire quickly. Everyone had to run out of the house, and they had watched the flames eat up their home. The men had laughed, and the women had been sad.

The following morning, Kukul remembered, moods had been reversed. The men had had long faces, and the women had bustled about trying to make corn patties in the open and packing up meager lunches. The men had taken their food packages silently and had quickly disappeared. They had spent all day in the forest, and had returned in the evening with new palm leaves for a roof, branches and withes for a house. It had taken them two days to build a new hut, but all the men of the compound had worked on it together and it had not been too bad a dwelling when it was finished. In some ways Kukul had liked the new house better than the old. It smelled of leaves and tree trunks, and for a few days it had seemed to whisper like the forest. But Kukul did not like sleeping in the open, which is what she had to do while the men were building the house. Lying in the compound at night, she could hear the coyotes howl, and everybody knew that coyotes were the epitome of evil.

Kukul also remembered the occasion as one of the few times in her life when her mother had punished her seriously. Usually, Kukul's mother was gentle and carefully explained why certain manners and ways had been adopted, tested and practiced over the years, and therefore deserved to be honored and obeyed. Kukul's father and two older brothers were less patient. When they thought Kukul had done something wrong, they would scold and pinch her ears. That one time, Kukul's mother had done worse. She had rubbed chili into Kukul's eyes and nose. It had stung and pained, and for days afterwards Kukul's eyes had smarted and her nose had itched.

Kukul had been punished with such severity because she got angry at the men for burning down the house during the festivities of the night, and in the morning had boldly asked her older brother why they did such things. The brother, a hunter by trade, who was skilled as well at making twine for ropes, sandals, bows and fishing lines, had not even deigned to reply. He had just glowered in fury and disgust at such an ignorant, irreverent question. But mother had heard Kukul, and told her afterwards that she had shown disrespect both to the men and the gods, and this could not be permitted. To make certain that Kukul would remember the injunction, mother had taken Kukul into a neighbor's kitchen and slowly, deliberately had rubbed the stinging chili into her face.

It was not a pleasant memory. Kukul shook her head several times to make it go away, and decided to think instead of the time of year just beginning, which was her favorite season. It was a time when the men of the compound were busy and happy, and away from the house for a large part of the day. They spent their days in the jungle, slashing and burning, to prepare new ground for the sowing of the corn. All around the city, there was the smell of smoke, with wisps of it floating in the distance. The wisps had pretty shapes—they seemed to repeat in the air forms they had had when they were leaves on the trees—and there was a mystery in the smell of things growing and dying and growing again.

Later in the season came the time for sowing and weeding. Finally, harvest time arrived, preceded by night-long prayer vigils at the compound's own small temple nearby. Being a girl, Kukul was not permitted to attend these evenings of worship, but the temple was close enough for her to hear the murmur of the men praying in chorus, in a deep singsong that sounded to Kukul like the voice of a river, flowing slowly, nourishing the land.

In Kukul's view the six months between the preparation of the fields in the rainforest, and the time the men came home carrying loads of corn, beans, squashes and pumpkins, was a period when everything was right with the world. The men of the compound left early in the morning in groups of twenty, to work together first the fields of the *halach uinic* and the priests, then each family's plot in turn. They greeted each other cheerfully at dawn and came home together in the evening tired and content.

It was different in the winter. The men stayed around the house and compound then, father whittling obsidian blades for knives, spears and offerings, younger brother carving woodbeams, older brother working his twine. The men soon got restless and sullen. Father's blades took on increasingly strange shapes as the winter wore on, became curved, twisted and weird looking. Some, Kukul thought, looked like profiles of the gods of the underworld.

In the winter, Kukul's younger brother would get mischievous and, instead of carving the glyphs and designs that had been ordered for the lintels of temples and palaces, he would start doodling, just putting down little pictures that came into his head. Kukul knew her younger brother well enough to be certain that ideas popping into his head were not always serious or respectful. Besides, it was a dangerous practice. If one of the architects examined the beam carefully enough to find a doodle, and got angry, Kukul's brother could wind up with a severe punishment that would disgrace the whole family. He might even be sentenced to slavery and they would all have to think of ways to work and skimp to buy him free again.

It was her older brother, the hunter, however, who worried Kukul most. He had a habit of suddenly getting up from his rope-making and, without a word to anyone, walking away and disappearing into the forest. He could be gone for days and they would wonder whether a jaguar had killed him or a snake had poisoned him. Sometimes, he came back from these trips with a tapir or an iguana, or a brace of wild turkeys. That was fine, but he had also returned one time with a mean gash, inflicted by a puma, that ran from his neck all the way to the small of his back. They had had to ask the *ah-men*, the priest-healer, to calm the fever that had gripped brother for weeks after the puma's attack. It had taken almost a year before the magic, the incantations and the herbs of the *ah-men* had finally produced a cure. The animal's mark was still there, spread out on brother's back like a pink-red poisonous plant.

Kukul's brother had confessed to the priest at the time that the attack was probably a punishment sent by the god of the hunters. He had killed a turkey without saying "*otzilen*"—"I am in need." Men were expected to apologize to the animals they were about to kill, and make clear that they were doing so out of need. The brother had failed to honor this traditional obligation when he had caught the turkey early in the day. That evening, a little deeper in the jungle, the puma had leaped at him. He was lucky to be alive. Kukul shuddered at the memory. It had been a bad winter.

Still, spring had come at last, that year and this. Today the men would be leaving right after breakfast. For the afternoon, Kukul's mother had invited friends to come and weave in the yard behind the house, where the ground had been trampled down evenly so that the looms could be set up without wobbling. Kukul liked it back there. The yard was rimmed by her mother's avocado grove on one side and a row of soapberry trees on the other. Between the yard and the forest, mother had another enclosure for her animals. She kept a dozen ducks with beautiful plumes, which she was raising for a special mantle and breechclout for the upcoming wedding of Kukul's older brother. At this time, the enclosure also contained two deer, a monkey, and half a dozen small, fat dogs. The dogs would be eaten in the winter, when there was little other meat to be had. Kukul did not like to see the dogs prepared for feasting. Alive, they were so warm and funny. Her brother the hunter had explained to her why they had to be eaten. The animals, he had told her, all animals, had had their chance at becoming masters of the world. The gods created them before man. But the animals could not speak, and therefore could not praise the lords of creation. The lords wanted to be praised. That is why they created man and gave him dominion over animals and vegetables. Now, Kukul's brother said, the vegetables sustain animals, and both nourish man so he can worship the gods.

Kukul enjoyed the afternoons spent with women weaving in the yard. The women talked a lot, laughed, and made lovely fabrics on their looms. Kukul's mother was particularly expert. She was known throughout Tikal for the beauty of her cloth. Her designs were traditional, but she had a special way with dyes, and her yarns emerged looking vivid and delicate at the same time. She also had a talent for adding small touches of her own to the traditional motifs. She would put an extra curve or swirl into a repeating pattern, an extra feature on a face, even a curving long tail on a star.

She had begun to embellish her stars after the family had watched a star one night streaking across the sky, with a long, golden tail fluttering behind it. The people of Tikal had been frightened by the phenomenon until the priest, after fasting for a week, had announced that it was a good omen. So it had proven to be. The harvest that season had been the best in years. Some of the ears of corn the men brought home that autumn had almost looked like the star's golden tail, especially when they had been stashed for safe storage in the *chultun,* the deep hole in the corner of the yard, all lined with lime and covered by a heavy lid. Before the lid of the *chultun* was lowered, the ears of corn had glinted in the dark like the tail of that streaking star in the sky. Ever since then, Kukul's mother had woven her stars with long curves attached to them. People said that Kukul's mother enjoyed the blessing of Ixchel, the goddess of weaving. Kukul had a special feeling of her own about Ixchel, who was the wife of Itzamna, the god of writing.

Kukul strained to hear what the family was doing. It was about time for them to rise. Her mother would be up first, to help with the baking of the corn patties for breakfast. Then the men would get dressed and go to the brook to wash before they sat down for the morning meal. They would have to be served quickly because from spring to fall they were always eager to leave. Kukul and her mother would not get a chance to eat until the men had left.

But no one was stirring yet. Listening attentively, Kukul could hear their deep, regular breaths mixed with an occasional snore. Good, she thought, that gives me time to daydream a little.

She settled back on her folded legs, moving the fan slowly, rhythmically over the glowing hearth. The fan threw shadows on the fire that came and went as she moved her hand.

The sky had looked like that on the day she first saw Itzamna, with the clouds seeming to play catch, running across the face of the sun. It had been the day of communion for both of them, her twelfth birthday, his fourteenth. With a score of other boys and girls, they had arrived with their parents just after dawn at the consecrated grounds before the temple, swept clean and strewn with fresh branches and leaves. The grounds had been roped off, with four wise old men guarding each corner. In the center of the grounds the officiating priest, resplendently dressed, had sat with a bowl of pure spring water in one hand, a jade staff in the other. One by one, the children had come before him to answer his questions and confess their sins.

Kukul had been terrified. Since she was small and shy, she had managed to hide herself at the very end of the line of girls. This had given her more time to think and be afraid. When her turn had come to face the priest, she had hardly been able to speak. But she had committed none of the sins he had asked her about, and the ordeal of looking into his stern face had been mercifully short. He had moistened her forehead with a few drops of the virgin water—it had felt cool and nice to Kukul—and had touched her with his staff. He had said nothing, but his eyes had seemed to tell a story of their own, an ancient tale of the Mayan people, of the first man and woman, and of all the men and women who had, through the ages, made and continued the Maya nation by respecting their rulers, obeying their priests, and worshiping the gods.

Later in the ceremony, when each of the girls and boys had confessed to the priest and been consecrated by him, he had said some of these things, pointing out also what it meant in daily duties to be a Mayan woman or a Mayan man, and how it was a demanding but also a wonderful way of life.

It was just before the priest had addressed them that Kukul first saw Itzamna. A problem had arisen during his confession. Apparently he had taken some actions, delved into certain mysteries, that he should not have probed at his age. But it emerged that he had done so under the guidance of his uncle, who was a priest, and his grandfather, who was a famous astronomer. This extraordinary behavior had to be explained and considered, and the officiating priest had told Itzamna to stand aside until he had spoken with all the other boys whose personal histories were less complicated. That is how it had happened that Kukul and Itzamna wound up at the end of their respective lines during the priest's final address. They had looked at each other once, then quickly lowered their eyes, as was proper. Thereafter, the words of the priest had commanded their attention and even though their eyes had never met again that day, Kukul had felt that the priest's words had spread over them like a canopy that would, somehow, cover her and Itzamna for the rest of their lives.

Later that day, Kukul's mother removed the red shell of her childhood, and Kukul's hair, which had been dressed in four little pigtails standing up like horns, was brushed out into two sleek plaits curving down her neck.

Women wore their hair in plaits after the initiation ceremony had officially made them adults. Later, after they were married, they could dress the hair, shape it into beehives and coronets, or pile it up in ringlets. Kukul's mother continued to wear her hair in braids, but other women Kukul had seen at the market had very elaborate hairstyles, which they kept in place with the sweet-smelling sap of the chicle tree, or the resin of amber.

Kukul's mother had her own ideas about beauty. As with her

weaving, she honored the traditions but was not altogether conventional. She had, for example, never put Kukul's head between two wooden boards when she was a baby to flatten the head into an elongated line. Nor had she dangled the traditional ball of resin between Kukul's eyes at the same time to permanently direct the gaze inward. Custom called for this and Kukul's mother had followed custom with all her other children: Kukul's two older sisters, who were married; her older brothers; and two of the three boys who had died so young that Kukul never knew them.

One brother had died of a stomach ailment. The *ah-men* said it was caused by black magic practiced against the boy by a man in the next compound. Kukul's brother had taken the family monkey for a walk and when they got to the next compound's beehive the monkey had decided to lunch on the honey and had so frightened the bees with his hairy paws that they never again gave good honey. The neighbors had not taken the matter to a judge because they felt the judge would not hold the boy responsible for the action of his monkey, particularly since at that time boy and monkey were about equal in size, with a little edge for the monkey. Certainly the monkey had been the stronger and more agile of the two. The neighbors therefore had said nothing in public—people would have felt that it would have been mean-spirited of them to do so—but they had been angry all the same. One dark night they had gone out to the forest with a bag full of bones and beans, and some strange herbs and powders, and one of them had practiced black magic against the boy under one of the wild cotton trees, which hold up the heavens. It had been a doubly wicked thing to do, to use a sacred *ceiba* for such a purpose. But it had also been doubly potent. The boy took ill the following morning and died less than a week later. He had been eight years old at the time and Kukul had not yet been born.

Kukul's other brother died when he was about the age she was now, just a little over twelve. His was a natural death. He was bitten by a poisonous snake while he was weeding the beans that were planted in the corn field so that they could be draped around the strong stalks of the maize for support. One bean plant had dropped to the ground and, as Kukul's brother reached to pull it up, a rattler that had been using the plant's leaves for shade put its fangs into the boy's hand. When his father had looked for him at lunchtime, after he had not answered the meal call, he had found the boy at the edge of the field, stiff, with his face and body a strange blue. It was almost like the sacred blue, Kukul's father had said, indicating what everyone knew anyhow: that children who die working, women who die in childbirth, or men who offer themselves as sacrifices, go straight to heaven.

The thought did not please Kukul. Her mother had almost gone to heaven when Kukul was only about three years old. That was when the last of the children was born, another boy. It had been a painful time for Kukul's mother. She was a woman with soft features that reminded Kukul of the face of the full moon. She moved lightly, like a deer. But at that particular time she had been heavy and awkward, and deep lines had marked her face. When the little boy finally came, the women of the compound had looked troubled, and the *ah-men* had said very little. For days no one knew whether mother would survive. Finally it was the little boy who had died, before the week was out. And mother had recovered.

That little boy's head had never been put between the flattening boards either, of course. Curled up, as he had been inside his mother, he had been placed into a large and lovely clay jar, painted by his father and brothers, and buried under the floor of the room in which he had been born. That way his spirit remained with the family and sometimes, when the men were away and the house was very still, Kukul thought she caught a glimpse of his little brown face in the shadow of a corner, or heard the gurgling sound he had made when once she tickled him with a leaf as he lay on his tiny grass mat shortly after he was born.

Kukul's head was as brown and round as the baby's had been. It troubled her sometimes, because a long head made a person look noble, and eyes turned to face each other imparted a thoughtful appearance. Itzamna's head and eyes were like that. He looked like the corn god. Her own eyes were round and gazed straight out at the world.

After the *emku* ceremony, where Kukul had first seen Itzamna, and had begun to wonder why she looked different from the other children, her mother had explained.

"Your name is Kukul," she had said, "the hummingbird. The hummingbird's head is round and its eyes look lustrously into the treetops. I want you to look and be like that bird all your life. A kukul is sweet and tranquil, and sings the song that is the heart of man. Its beauty is in its spirit and its voice. And it is small, like you."

Kukul's mother did concede that the hummingbird also had lovely, many-colored feathers and, after the *emku* ceremony, she had allowed Kukul to have her teeth filed and inlaid with shell and colored stones, to wear earrings of coral, use a dab of amber resin on her forehead, and carry a nosegay of flowers whenever she left the house.

Kukul's mother must have had some special counsel from the gods, perhaps from her protectress Ixchel, that made her decide to leave Kukul's appearance so unconventional. Itzamna liked Kukul's looks. The thought brought a flush to Kukul's cheeks—or perhaps the pink glow that suffused her face was caused by the heat of the hearth which was becoming increasingly intense. Itzamna, too, had said that Kukul looked like a hummingbird. He had added that this was of special significance because his own profession, writing, was an attempt to capture through memory the words of the gods, while hummingbirds sang the thoughts of men. He and Kukul therefore had tasks that fitted well together and would make for a harmonious life.

Kukul knew about all this because her brother, the hunter, had told her father one evening when Kukul was in the kitchen preparing the evening meal with her mother. The men, talking in the living room, did not think that the women would overhear their conversation. Itzamna had contrived to have Kukul's brother take him on one of his more adventurous trips into the forest. For several days the two had set traps for animals, hunted birds with clay pellets from their slingshots and blowguns, and had caught a tapir with their spears. Both were wearing tapir sandals now, as Kukul had had occasion to notice when she saw Itzamna a week earlier, on his way to the school where they taught him writing, calendrics and astronomy.

Kukul had been on her way to market with her mother, who was taking a particularly pretty piece of cloth she had woven to the tradesman who sold the cloth for her. Before they had set out that morning, Kukul and her mother had made up a small nosegay, with the color of the flowers in it repeating the colors of the pattern in the cloth. Kukul had known she looked pretty because her ankle-length chemise, of delicate white cotton, had an embroidered border that also matched the nosegay. When Kukul and Itzamna had passed each other on the causeway, they had both quickly looked away—Kukul had turned her face aside and Itzamna had stared straight ahead holding his head high—but for the rest of the day Kukul had felt like living up to her name by warbling out loud. She did not do so until they got back home, but once there, her mother had assured her that it was all right for her to feel like singing. After all, she was a kukul.

Kukul had never before talked to her mother about Itzamna, but that evening, after she overheard the conversation between her father and her brother, Kukul's hands had not been their usual quick and clever selves. Her mother had noticed. Some of Kukul's corn patties had come out heavy and lumpy that evening, but she had not minded eating those herself, as custom required. Her mother had given her a beaker full of wild cherry juice to wash them down. Kukul had thanked her mother with her eyes and neither had spoken a word. But Kukul knew that her mother had understood what was in her heart, and was thinking about it.

The family was stirring in the inner rooms, and for the rest of that morning Kukul had no time for daydreams or memories. First, the ducks, the deer, the dogs and the monkey had to be fed, given water and washed—when they could be persuaded to let themselves be washed. Kukul was the only one in the family who could accomplish that task without the dogs yapping and the monkey setting up a howl. The animals liked Kukul, and she liked them. She enjoyed watching the way they moved, each animal in its own characteristic way: the waddle of the ducks, the deer who moved like dancers, the gawky, cuddly walk of the dogs—each one reminded Kukul of a baby trying out its first steps—and, of course, the fast and fancy antics of the monkey who could lope, jump, and swing from tree branches. The monkey quite often put on an acrobatic performance for Kukul, particularly when it saw her come into the yard with a bowl of water and a root of the soapberry tree. That combination, the monkey knew, meant a scrubbing, and he would not let anyone do it except Kukul—occasionally. The monkey knew Kukul would do it gently.

Kukul sometimes wondered why the animals disliked being washed. She enjoyed her visits to the compound steambath, where certain hours of the morning were set aside for women. She would have preferred it if her family had been able to afford a private bath. In fact, a steambath of her own, and hair dressed in a cap of ringlets, were Kukul's ideas of real, grown-up luxury. However, she considered any kind of washing a pleasure, almost a privilege.

Kukul had been taught very early in life that water was precious. It nourished the fields and the trees, her mother had pointed out, and made it possible for corn and pumpkins, squashes and chili—and their own avocado and soapberry trees—to grow.

Kukul also remembered the many nights when the men of the family had gone to the nearby temple to pray from dusk to dawn. Their prayers in most of these vigils were addressed to Chac, the god of rain. Sometimes the men asked the big crocodile, which lived in the water, to give up some of its liquid resources. When Chac and the crocodile were slow to respond, and the fields began to look parched, the men took honeyfire with them to cajole the gods and put them in a good mood. At such times Kukul and her mother also prepared food for the deities, special dishes covered with flavorful sauces, or offerings that contained honey and vanilla, so that the sweetness and fragrance would please Chac. As far back as Kukul could remember, the gods had been pleased, sooner or later, with the gifts and had sent the needed water. Sometimes they sent it in good measure and at the right time, sometimes they provided it more scantily and late in the season. Occasionally they even supplied too much of it, and that was not desirable. It drowned the young shoots of the corn. When that happened, Kukul recalled, the men went to the temple of the jaguar, in the heart of the city, and asked that powerful king of the forests to intercede with the gods and have them stop the rain so that man and animal would not be swept away by a flood.

The animals understood the peril of floods. Way back, at the beginning of the world's creation, all animals had once been swallowed up in a flood, when they would not, or perhaps could not, use their voices to praise the gods. The gods got angry then, and swept away the animals in a great deluge.

Whenever Kukul thought about that, her heart become confused. She hated to think of all these animals dying in the flood. But if it had not been for that flood, the gods would never have made human beings, out of a golden kernel of corn, and then she would not exist, or her parents and brothers and sisters—or Itzamna.

That last thought settled Kukul's confusion. It was better that the gods had done what they did, way back there in the beginning.

Kukul's next task, after feeding and washing the animals, was to sweep the house. She did this with a hard broom made of rushes and twigs. Then she cleaned and cooled floor and walls by sprinkling them with fresh water, which her brother had fetched from the city reservoir the night before. It had been kept overnight in a large brown jar that looked and smelled like fresh earth. Kukul had used some of the water earlier to wash the breakfast dishes, scraping off the remains of chili and corn with a root of the soapberry tree.

Her house chores completed, Kukul joined her mother in the

yard. Together, they watered the groves, the glistening green avocado bushes, and the taller, gray-green soapberry trees. They also washed some clothes. The bulk of the laundry was done once a week, when all the women of the compound got together and made a party of it. Kukul liked the sounds of laundry day in the compound: the splashing of the water, the snapping of the cotton garments, the laughter of the ladies. She also liked the sight and smell of the mantles and breechclouts of the men, and the chemises of the women, drying on the special plot of grass set aside for the purpose. Just washed, the cotton shone white on the green, and smelled of grass, sun, and soapberry.

Once in a while, a little laundry had to be done between the weekly washfest. This happened when the men got too many of their cotton capes muddy in the fields, or when Kukul's mother decided, as she had that morning, that she and her daughter should have fresh chemises for the day.

Kukul and her mother had a busy morning. Lunch, consisting of corn patties left over from breakfast, an avocado pear they found lying under its bush, plump, soft, and creamy, and a drink of wild cherry juice, was delicious but brief. They still had some spinning to do, to get their threads ready for the weaving of the afternoon.

Like all Mayan girls, Kukul had learned to spin when she was very young, just old enough to hold a spindle and twirl it. It had become almost as automatic a part of her existence as breathing. Whenever there was nothing else to do, Mayan women spun. Kukul had seen women going to market, carrying their shopping baskets on an A-frame strapped to their backs, and using their hands to spin on the way. This was true especially when the women lived on the far outer rim of the city and had to come a long distance. During the summer season, before the rains, Kukul and her mother usually did their spinning under the shade of the tallest of their soapberry trees, leaning against the trunk in companionable silence.

Spinning under the soapberry tree that afternoon, Kukul's mind wandered. What would it be like to be married to Itzamna? To live in a big house that was not rounded at the edges but stretched out, long and elegant, its outer wall covered with white limestone and painted in brilliant colors, and another wall inside, dividing living and sleeping areas, also painted with gay and delicate designs? Such a house, Kukul knew, had its entrance covered not by a grass mat like her own home, but with a woven curtain of featherwork, multi-colored and fluffy, with strings of melodious copper bells on each side, which visitors touched to announce themselves. In such a house, meals were served in beautiful dishes set on embroidered cotton mats, and people took their ease on colored cushions placed on wooden stools instead of plain grass mats on the floor.

What would it be like, Kukul wondered, to raise doves and bees in her own garden? And in that garden to have a small pool which she would get ready for Itzamna's bath each morning by dropping a steaming stone into the water to make it tepid and just right for bathing? What would it be like, while she was serving fine meals with special spices or cool drinks in lovely beakers, to listen to Itzamna talking with his father who made these marvelous journeys, or his uncle the priest who could explain the mysteries of conversing with gods? Or, best of all, to his grandfather, that wise man with the white hair growing from his chin and the large eyes that shone like the stars he had been watching, out there in the forest, for longer than anyone in her family could remember? What would it be like to hear Itzamna open the fan of his parchment and read what the gods had permitted him to remember that day of the history of the Maya, their traditions, their customs, their calculations, and perhaps even their future which doubled back in a circle to the past?

It would, Kukul decided, be a lovely life.

Her mother's voice broke into her reveries.

"The gods take their work seriously. We must do the same."

Kukul's mother spoke gently, but seriously. Had she been traveling with Kukul in her thoughts? Kukul's mother seemed capable of doing that. She often surprised Kukul by picking up a thought or a dream that was floating through Kukul's mind, and either carrying the dream to a practical conclusion or commenting on the thought. She was doing so now, speaking of marriage, its duties and obligations.

Kukul, her mother pointed out, would be expected to bear eight children, and carefully raise those whom the gods would choose to let live. She would have to obey her husband at all times, even if she thought he was doing something wrong, and she would have to show respect for him even when he was drunk and silly, as all men sometimes were.

Looking after a house, grove and garden was not easy, Kukul's mother noted, and became more complicated and demanding when the house was larger and its furnishings richer, even with servants to help. Kukul would be responsible for the home. She would have to supervise servants and pay attention to many more things than she did now, and would have little time for her favorite occupation of letting her thoughts fly. Kukul's mother did not object to this occupation. She thought it fitting for a girl whose name and spirit was that of a hummingbird.

But Kukul's mother did remind her daughter that the gods, in one of their early creations, had made the stones and clays of the earth into living beings, and had relegated them to their present inferior status only when it was discovered that they could not speak and sing the gods' praises. Stones and clays, however, still remembered the days when they had been the lords of the earth, and sometimes became resentful of man whom they now had to serve. They showed this resentment through rebellion, Kukul's mother explained, all kinds of rebellions that could upset the day of a wife: dishes chipping, *metates* tilting, even a hearth suddenly collapsing for no reason at all. Implements did such things, and a wife had to understand, and be prepared to deal with them and their perversities with sympathy and patience. They did not, after all, lead a pleasant life, having been demoted from their days of glory to become the servants of man. They had a right to be angry every now and then.

Kukul had noticed that implements were indeed angry with her quite frequently, more frequently than they were with her mother. But then her mother treated them with more care and attention than Kukul did, who thought them hard and ugly. Perhaps if she had more beautiful implements, Kukul speculated, she would love them more and treat them better.

The arrival of the ladies put an end to Kukul's flights of fancy. It turned out to be an exciting afternoon, with many patterns taking shape on the looms, and the sounds of the shuttles providing counterpoint to the stories the ladies had to tell.

One lady reported how a special dish she had prepared for the big sacrifices of the previous day had really pleased the gods. The minute her husband had put it down near the altar, a flame had leaped over it and swallowed it up. The lady had put the last of their vanilla and cacao beans into the dish and, as the flame consumed it, a sweet-smelling smoke had floated up to tickle the nostrils of the deities. Clearly the gods had been pleased with the offering, and her husband had been very attentive to her all day. He had even stopped off at one of the jewelry stalls on his way home from the temple to buy her an ornament for the left nostril. It was a disk fashioned of bits of jade, coral and mother-of-pearl. She was wearing it, and the other ladies were lavish in their admiration. Kukul's mother suggested to the woman that she weave a fabric with the same colors as the nose ring: green, pale red, and silvery white. She promised to help the lady prepare the dyes.

Another weaver with good news was a woman known for her expertise as a pottery maker. She shaped rings of orange clay into vessels, building them up by piling ring upon ring, then molding, firing and painting them. Her specialty were censers, the large ones used for the burning of *pom* on special occasions such as communions and weddings, births and funerals. It took a great deal of time and skill to make these censers, but they also fetched a very good price. She had sold six on new year's day and had come home with a big bag of cacao beans, plus three chains of copper bells. She was feeling proud, and it was difficult for her that afternoon to maintain the attitude of modesty that was expected of a Mayan lady at all times. The women understood how she felt. Having a bag full of cacao beans at home was a fine, luxurious feeling, and having earned it oneself was no mean achievement.

Not all the weavers' stories were happy ones, however. One of the ladies had discovered that two of her dogs had strayed from the yard during the night, and the coyotes had caught and consumed them. There had been nothing left of the dogs in the morning but a few scattered bones.

Another lady was deeply troubled by her son who had made a false step in the most important of yesterday's dance rituals, and the priests were very angry with him. The gods considered such inattention offensive, and the boy's misbehavior might well bring bad fortune to all the people of Tikal. The priests were considering whether the boy should become a slave so that the gods would be appeased, and some of the sterner priests were even hinting darkly at sacrificing the negligent dancer. It would probably not come to that, but the boy certainly was in serious trouble and his mother was worried and unhappy. She tried to concentrate on her weaving, an intricate piece of cloth with a very old pattern, which she intended to send to the temple as soon as it was finished. Her hope was that it would make the gods, and the priests, forgive the transgression of her son. She was working intensely, and had vowed to stay at her loom until the cloth was finished, however long it took. Her fellow-weavers expressed their sympathy but did not offer to help. They knew that for the cloth to be acceptable to the gods in the way the woman wanted, it would have to be the product of her own hard effort.

For Kukul, the afternoon that had begun so pleasantly ended in sadness. It happened when one of the ladies spoke of her son who was about to be married. The boy's father had engaged an *ah-atan-zahob* a few weeks' earlier and the lady was very appreciative of the negotiations this marriage broker had conducted on behalf of the groom. The *ah-atanzahob* had arranged for the groom to work the customary three years for his father-in-law, instead of the four years that the bride's parents had originally requested. For their part, the groom's parents had been persuaded to do a little better than usual in the matter of the bride price, adding an extra five lengths of cotton, three sacks of corn, and two bags of cacao beans. The girl was worth it. She was known to be one of the best weavers in the town, as well as an excellent cook.

They were getting ready for the wedding now, the groom's mother told her friends, and she expected them all at the festivities to come. A priest had already been engaged to bless the new couple, and an astrologer to forecast its future. In Mayan society, weddings were arranged by the groom's parents, who provided everything for the occasion, including the bridal gown. The cloth the lady was working was the fringed shawl of the wedding dress which the girl would wear over her hair as a bride, draped across her shoulders as a wife.

The talk of marriage negotiations frightened Kukul. Itzamna, being a scribe, would not be able to come and work for her father, who could certainly use an extra pair of hands. Also, Itzamna's family might well object to their son marrying Kukul. They were a distinguished family, of a higher class. Itzamna's father was a rich merchant, held in considerable esteem by the rulers of Tikal. His mother was the daughter of a provincial governor, whose own parents had been none too happy when she married out of the minor nobility to which her family belonged. They might think the marriage of Itzamna and Kukul another social comedown.

Besides, Kukul wondered painfully, how could she deprive her own family of the valuable services of a son-in-law? With three brothers dead, they were already a small family, short of men. Kukul felt her heart hammer, then stand still. Her shuttle missed and clattered to the ground. As she reached in embarrassment to retrieve it, Kukul saw her mother look up for an instant from an almost-finished piece of cloth.

Kukul's mother spoke almost immediately after the last of the ladies had folded her loom, strapped it to the carrying frame on her back, and left. The two were in the kitchen then, preparing the stacks of corn patties for which their hungry menfolk would be clamoring as soon as they got home. Fanning once again the embers of the hearth, Kukul had made up her mind that she could not marry Itzamna. His family would not allow it and, as a dutiful daughter, she could not ask her father to forego the services of a son-in-law. Tears welled up in her eyes. They fell into the ashes and died there with a hissing sound.

"It will not be easy," Kukul's mother said, as if she had heard all of her daughter's musings. "The negotiations will take long, and many problems will have to be solved. But Itzamna's mother knows how important it is to be married to the person you love, even if difficulties have to be overcome to arrange it. We can ask for a bigger bridal price to compensate for the loss of Itzamna's services. That will not be difficult for Itzamna's family. And your father will manage, with your brothers and the other men of the compound. He wants to see you happy. After all, you are a kukul, and we must all do what we can to help your spirit soar and sing."

Kukul looked up at her mother and the gloom that had enveloped her lifted and disappeared, like one of those storm-laden clouds of the rainy season chased by a strong wind.

"Yes," she thought, "I am a kukul. I can fly. I feel like flying now."

The tears stopped. There was no more hissing in the ashes and the embers of the hearth began to glow, rosy and reassuring.

Kukul's mother spoke again.

"Anyway," she said, "you will have to wait at least another two years before you can get married. And Itzamna must reach the age of eighteen before he can do so. Four years is a very long time."

It did not seem so to Kukul, even though four years represented one third of the span she had lived thus far. She would use the time to learn perfectly everything a Mayan wife should know. She would catch a glimpse of Itzamna sometimes, at the market perhaps, or on the causeway near her house, when he went out to the forest to visit his grandfather. She would hear about him, too. Kukul knew that Itzamna would see to that. The four years would pass quickly.

The fire was up now, crackling and beautiful. Kukul joined her mother, broke off a piece of corn dough, flattened it carefully between her hands, and tossed it from one palm to the other in an arc almost as high and even as her mother's. In the distance, she heard voices and the fall of feet on the causeway. The men of the compound were coming home.

MAJOR MAYA SITES
AND
MUSEUM COLLECTIONS

In Guatemala:

Tikal, in the north-eastern rainforest of Guatemala, reportedly means "where the voices of the departed are heard"—and indeed they are. It is a magnificent site of temples and palaces, courts, stelae, altars, tombs and their contents, reservoirs, causeways and house-mounds, all from the classic period. At that time, Tikal seems to have been a Maya Athens, a major—perhaps even *the* major—city-state of the Maya realm.

Tikal has a small but exquisite museum with a beautiful collection of glazed and painted pottery, jewelry of jade, coral and shell, and incised bones.

Other important sites in Guatemala (they can all be reached by road or airplane from Guatemala City) are: *Uaxactun, Quirigua, Zaculeu, Utatlan,* and *Kaminaljuyu,* the last on the outskirts of Guatemala City.

Guatemala City has a museum of archeology and anthropology, with a rich collection of Mayan artifacts in its show rooms, and an even richer one in its crowded basement.

In Honduras:

Copan, in north-western Honduras was, apparently, a scientific center for the Maya during the classic period. Copan has the famous Altar Q, with its congress of scientists carved around the rim; the rare stele showing a woman *halach uinic;* a handsome, well-preserved ball-court; the unique hieroglyphic stairway, with its 2,500 glyphs carved on steps and balustrades; fascinating temple ruins; and a rare collection of stelae carved in the round and in high relief.

A museum near the site, at *Santa Rosa de Copan,* has realistically modeled Mayan faces, including a woman and a teen-ager with curly hair who look as if they lived next door.

The museum also has animals sculptured by the classic Maya, including a wild turkey, a turtle, and a frog, the last looking so full, fat and wet that one expects it to jump out of its glass case at any moment.

The glass cases also contain interesting flint tools and obsidian blades.

In Mexico:

Uxmal, in the Yucatan Peninsula, is a lovely example of the Puuc style of Mayan architecture, dating just after the classic period. Its buildings include the handsome Governors' Palace; one of those nests of temples built on top of each other; and the famous "nunnery" quadrangle with its abstractions, in pastel-hued marbles and polished stones, of Maya deities, social classes, and dwelling places.

Chichen Itza, also in Yucatan, is an awesome example of Maya civilization under Toltec influence, when gentleness was turned to prowess, and the quest for harmony became a thirst for conquest. Castles and temples demonstrate the transformation and its results. They include such manifestations as the *chac mol*, a stone figure with a round head and empty, staring eyes, designed to hold the human sacrifice whose heart was offered to the god of war; and the "skull rack," where the heads of captives were stacked like bottles to dry in the sun, so that they could be ground into calcium to reinforce the concrete used in the construction of castles.

Chichen Itza also has a ballcourt, an interesting contrast in size, and the ferocious scenes sculpted on its walls, to the serene loveliness of the ballcourt at Copan; and the remains of a market, to date the only Mayan market extant.

Bonampak has the temple in which the famous murals were discovered. However, these can be seen more clearly, and in greater detail, in an excellent recreation at the Museum of Archeology in Mexico City, which also has a fine collection of other Maya treasures.

In the United States, the following museums have interesting Maya collections:

The Peabody Museum of Harvard University.

The University Museum of the University of Pennsylvania.

The Chicago Natural History Museum.

The American Museum of Natural History in New York.

The Museum of the American Indian in New York.

The Metropolitan Museum in New York.

SOME BOOKS TO READ

The Maya in History:

Bancroft, Hubert Howe. *History of Central America.* San Francisco: A.L. Bancroft & Co., 1883.

Coe, Michael D. *The Maya.* New York: Frederick A. Praeger, 1966.

Gann, Thomas. *Glories of the Maya.* New York: Scribners, 1939.

Gallenkamp, Charles. *Maya: The Riddle and Rediscovery of a Fabulous Civilization.* New York: Pyramid Publications, Inc., 1961.

Morley, Sylvanus Griswold. *The Ancient Maya.* Rev. by George W. Brainerd, Stanford, California: Stanford University Press, 1946.

Thompson, J. Eric S. *The Rise and Fall of Maya Civilization.* University of Oklahoma Press, 1954.

————. *The Civilization of the Maya.* Chicago: Chicago Natural History Museum Press, 1927.

The Maya Today:

La Farge, Oliver. *The Year Bearer's People.* Tulane Univ., 1931.

Mediz Bolio, Antonio. *The Land of the Pheasant and the Deer,* ill. by Diego Rivera. Mexico City: Editorial "Cultura," 1935.

Oakes, Maud. *Beyond the Windy Place.* New York: Farrar Straus Co., 1951.

————. *The Two Crosses of Todos Santos.* New York: Pantheon Books, Inc., 1951.

Samayoa Chinchilla, Carlos. *The Emerald Lizard*. Indian Hills, Col.: The
   Falcons Wing Press, 1957.

Travel in Maya Territory:

   Lorang, Sister Mary Corde. *Footloose Scientist in Mayan America*. New
      York: Scribners, 1966.

   Stephens, John Lloyd. *Incidents of Travel in Central America, Chiapas,
      and Yucatan*. New York: Harper Bros. 1843. This is a wonderful
      book by the first United States ambassador to the Central American
      Federation, available with original engravings and drawings by
      F. Catherwood as well as in an inexpensive, modern edition.

Historic Sources:

   Idell, Albert. *The Bernal Diaz Chronicles*. New York: Doubleday Dolphin,
      1956.

   Tozzer, A.M. *Bishop Landa's "Relacion de los cosas de Yucatan."*
      Cambridge, 1941.

Original Maya Sources:

   Chonay, Dionisio Jose. *Title of the Lords of Totonicapan*, trans. by Delia
      Goetz. Univ. of Oklahoma Press, 1953.

   Recinos, Adrian. *Popol Vuh, The Sacred Book of the Ancient Quiche
      Maya*. University of Oklahoma Press, 1950.

   ———. *The Annals of the Cakchiquels*, trans. by Delia Goetz. University
      of Oklahoma Press, 1953.

   Roys, R.L. *The Book of Chilam Balam of Chumayel*. Washington, D.C.:
      Carnegie Institution of Washington, 1933.

GLOSSARY

A Note on Pronunciation

a is pronounced ah, as in *a*rt

e is pronounced ay, as in *e*nd

i is pronounced ee, as in *i*s

o is pronounced oh, as in p*o*t

u is pronounced oo, as in b*u*ll

x is pronounced sh, as in *sh*adow

j is pronounced h', as in the Scottish lo*ch*

ch is pronounced as in *ch*ildren, not as in choral

All vowels are pronounced separately, as in chaos.

AH-ATANZAHOB (*Ah-Ah-tun-zah-hohb*)—Marriage broker.

AH-KIN (*Ah-Keen*)—The words mean "he, of the Sun." The *ah-kin* was the parish priest, mainly occupied with ritual.

AH-KULEKOB (*Ah-Koo-lay-kohb*)—Counselor to the ruler of a city-state, chosen for his specific expertise.

AH-MEN (*Ah-Mayn*)—The words mean "he who understands." The *ah-men* was a combination of healer, soothsayer and counselor in domestic matters.

AHUACAN *(Ah'-wua-kahn)*–High priest. The word means "the Lord Serpent." To the Maya, the serpent was the symbol of fertility, the energy of life.

BALAM *(Bah-lahm)*–Jaguar. To the Maya the jaguar was a symbol of power.

BALCHE *(Bahl-chay)*–A fermented drink distilled from honey. The Maya used it for festive occasions.

BATAB *(Bah-tahb)*–Provincial governor.

CHAC *(Chahk)*–Elder who served a religious function, especially in community rituals.

CHAC MOL *(Chahk mohl)*–A stone figure molded to hold human sacrificial victims. The *chac mol* is characteristic of the Toltec civilization and was introduced into Mayan culture in the late, "Mexican" period.

CENOTE *(Tsay-noh-tay)*–A sacrificial well, in which human victims were drowned to appease the rain god. The practice was introduced to the Mayan civilization during the Mexican period.

CHILAN *(Chee-lahn)*–The word means messenger. A *chilan* was a priest who interpreted the intentions of the gods to man, a combination prophet and diviner.

CHULTAN *(Chool-tahn)*–A Maya cellar, ranging in size from a limestone-lined hole in the ground to a series of underground chambers lined with plaster. The Maya stored food in these cellars.

CUCH CABOB *(Kooch-Cah-bohb)*–Municipal counselor.

EMKU *(Aym-koo)*–An initiation ceremony marking entry into adult life. Girls went through this ceremony when they were 12 years old, boys at age 14.

HALACH UINIC *(Hah-lahch Oo-neek)*–It means "true man" and was the designation conferred on the ruler of a Mayan city-state who was both the religious and temporal chief of the community.

HETZMEK *(Hayts-meyk)*–The earliest initiation ceremony in the life of a Maya child. It took place when a girl was three months old, a boy four months.

HOLPOPOB *(Hohl-poh-pohb)*–Local representative. The Maya equivalent to the Scandinavians' ombudsman.

KATUN *(Kah-toon)*–The period at which the Mayas' three calendars—the religious, the natural and the mathematical—coincided. This happened every 260 years and the Maya believed that each *katun* constituted a cycle in human history.

MAYAB *(Mah-yahb)*–Deriving from *ma* meaning no, and *yab*, meaning many, adds up to "the not many." One theory has it that *Maya* is a shortening of *Mayab*, meaning, in context, the select few.

MILPA *(Meel-pub)*–A field of maize.

NACOM *(Nah-cohm)*–Military leader, elected for three years.

OTZILEN *(Oh-tsee-layn)*–The words mean "I am in need," and were addressed by the Maya, as an explanation and apology, to animals they killed for food.

POK-TO-POK *(Pohk-toh-pohk)*–The Maya ball game, which had ritual meaning in addition to being a sports event. *Pok-to-pok* is an onomatopoeic word reflecting the sound of the hard rubber ball used in the game on the stone floor of the ball court.

POM *(pohm)*–Mayan incense, still used.

POPOL VUH *(Poh-pohl-Vooh)*–Literally translated, it would mean the Book of Council or the Book of the Community. It is the sacred text of Maya beliefs and origins, comparable to the Old Testament.

TUN *(Toon)*–The calendar year.

TUPIL *(Too-peel)*–Policeman.

UINAL *(Uee-nahl)*–The Maya day in the astronomical sense, i.e. the 24-hour cycle.

Important Place Names

ATITLÁN–*(Ah-teet-lahn')*

BONAMPAK–*(Boh-nahm-pahk')*

CHICHÉN ITZÁ–*(Chee-Chayn' Eet-zah')*

COPÁN–*(Koh-pahn')*

KAMINALJUYÚ–*(Kah-meen-ahl-h'oo-yoo')*

PALENQUE–*(Pah-layn'-kay)*

PIEDRAS NEGRAS–*(Pee-ay'-drahs Nay'-grahs)*

QUIRIGUÁ–*(Kee-ree-gwah')*

TIKAL–*(Tee-kahl')*

UAXACTÚN–*(Wah-shahk-toon')*

UXMAL–*(Oosh-mahl')*

ZACULEU–*(Zah-koo-lay'-ooh)*

INDEX